echoes
choes
hoes
oes
es
s

Compiled by Jim Kacian & Julie Warther

echoes 2

Red Moon Press © 2018
Poems are copyrighted in the names of the individual poet.
All rights revert to the poet upon publication.

Red Moon Press
P.O. Box 2461
Winchester VA
22504-1661 USA
www.redmoonpress.com

ISBN 978-1718615854

Though extensive, this volume is far from complete.
We have tried to contact every poet from every volume of *New Res*,
but as you will discover, we have not always been successful.
We could use your help.
If you know any of the poets who do not have an updated page here,
please contact them and let them know we'd love to hear from them.
It is our hope that this book will evolve over time.

A free online version of *echoes* 2 is available at
https://www.thehaikufoundation.org/omeka/items/show/5495

Foreword to *echoes* 1

Somewhere midway through the third of what is now five volumes (and counting) of *The New Resonance* series it became apparent to us that this was more than just a collection of books showcasing emerging talent. The New Resonance Poets are a community, and we wanted that community to stay in touch with each other and abreast of each other's work. The result is this volume, which is both a kind of yearbook and a compendium of outstanding work. It is also an almanac of the current state of affairs in English-language haiku, since so many who have appeared in this series have become the outstanding figures of our time in our genre, as poets, volunteers, speakers, officials, judges and most generally as the face of haiku today. We're proud of our role in identifying and nurturing this talent, but of course the credit ultimately must go to this talented group who have given us the opportunity to enjoy their work both in *The New Resonance* series and through their subsequent excellent appearances in journals and books worldwide. It is not too much to expect that we will look back at this group as seminal in the development of haiku in our time, and we have had the pleasure of seeing them grow into the role.

Jim Kacian & Dee Evetts
Series Editors, *A New Resonance*

Foreword to *echoes* 2

The *New Resonance* series celebrated its 20th anniversary with the publication of its 10th volume in 2017, bringing the New Resonance community to 170 poets, many of whom have made a serious impact on the practice of English-language haiku.

Following its fifth *New Res* volume, Red Moon Press produced *echoes 1*, which was an update of poets who appeared in those first five volumes. *echoes 2* brings the community up to date by including poets from all 10 volumes. It is a chance to touch base with our New Resonance friends — a reunion of sorts.

Of course, reunions can be tricky. We wonder what others' expectations are for us and whether we've met them. We've aged, changed, and hopefully grown. Our interests of five, ten or twenty years ago are different now. Those changes don't make us more or less a part of the community though. In this community, we know at some point haiku played a vital role in each poet's life. Its influence shaped, in large and small ways, who we are today. And these are the faces with which we look forward to getting reacquainted.

While all the members featured here share a love of haiku, they are also a wonderfully diverse group of individuals. Find in these pages a poet who teaches a course on cave painting and another who has had her tanka sequences performed by chorales. One lives off the grid. There are painters, photographers, singers, farmers, naturalists, homemakers, yoga instructors, teachers, writers, translators. Some who write everyday. Some who haven't written in years. Some who have recently returned to haiku after a long absence. Others who claim they may never write again. Many who have used these little poems to write through grief and illness or address social justice issues. We share the joy of finding the perfect words to express the heartfelt. We support each other and learn from our differences. This is the stuff of community.

To my fellow New Resonance poets... It has been a humbling experience working on *echoes 2*. In the process, I've had the pleasure of meeting some of you for the first time and hearing your stories. From one of the new kids in the neighborhood, thank you for showing me around and introducing me to your friends. For paving the way and sharing your lives. It has indeed been an honor and privilege.

> Julie Warther
> *A New Resonance* 9 Alumna
> Series Editor

---

10 volumes, 170 poets, 2550 poems over 20 years — *New Res* is a testament to the force of the flow that is English-language haiku. What began as a one-off has attained an arc and impetus of its own. Our series has become multi-generational, a bridge for people who share a language but no longer much of a culture. It is one way in which we affirm common cause, common values, a common poetic. Even this changes over time, and *New Res* is a testament to that as well. It is good to keep in touch, to share what's new and important in our lives, even if only occasionally, and even if we might have drifted away from that which once united us. We still want to hear how you've been. Thanks for letting us know.

> Jim Kacian
> Series Editor, *A New Resonance*
> and for 20-year fellow-editor Dee Evetts
> and for *echoes 1* co-compiler Alice Frampton

echoes
choes
hoes
oes
es
s

The Community

Name Scott Abeles
Volume *A New Resonance* 10
Residence Washington DC
Occupation Attorney

I'm just a simple poet. My awards and other honors include having work selected for several *Red Moon Anthologies*.

everywhere
but the road I'm on . . .
moonshine
Shamrock

a handgun found
among my father's things . . .
autumn begins
Modern Haiku

no matter how I try to dilute you absinthe
Frogpond 37.2

reawakening inside her rib cage murmur of autumn
Modern Haiku 46.2

just when I thought
she was out of my head
lilacs
Frogpond

city limits
the wind whispers
what I want it to
unpublished

Name **Mary Frederick Ahearn**
Volume ***A New Resonance* 10**
Residence **Pottstown PA**
Occupation **Retired**

I don't really have a haiku career, just a love for it and haibun. I also write tanka and tanka prose. No published books, just appearances in other people's books such as Robert Epstein, Scott Mason, and others. I've been included in *Red Moon Anthologies* for haiku and haibun, and won a Touchstone Individual Haiku Award from The Haiku Foundation in 2015.

mockingbird's song
again then again
he changes his tune
Acorn 39

sky mirrors sea
the morning after
a taste of salt
Modern Haiku 48:3

blank journals
the one
with flowers
Frogpond 40.3

honeybees sway
on the snowdrops
one of her good days
The Wonder Code

butterfly
on a dandelion
the baby's laugh
The Wonder Code

where the snow melts first snowdrops
Acorn 38

Name Melissa Allen
Volume *A New Resonance* 8
Residence Madison WI
Occupation Technical Writer

I'm currently a co-editor both of *Bones: journal of contemporary haiku* and of *Haibun Today*. I've been anthologized widely, including in *Haiku in English* (Norton, 2013), the *Red Moon Anthology* (2014 and 2016), and *Haiku 2014* and *Haiku 2016* (Modern Haiku Press). I've contributed haiku, haibun, haiga, and reviews to *Frogpond*, *Modern Haiku*, and several other journals, and an article to *Juxtapositions* (The Haiku Foundation, 2016). I presented at the Haiku North America conference in 2015 and 2017. At the moment, I'm more interested in writing haibun than standalone haiku. I live in Madison, Wisconsin, where I've been for 26 years after an upbringing in Connecticut. I work as a technical writer at a software company. It's more fun than it sounds. I have a grown son and two cats. When I'm not writing for fun or profit, I enjoy running, studying cloud formations, going to the theater, and making it up as I go along.

another bird dream probing the tenderness under a wing
    Frogpond 36.1

wind from the north a new piercing
    Modern Haiku 45.2

between the subtitles it's all nature
    is/let 9/2014

all the after of a rose remaining
    Frogpond 38.1

at dusk the cries of a flock of consonants
    moongarlic 6

tonight's moon another mistranslation
    Red Dragonfly: Haiku 2016

Name **Mike Andrelczyk**
Volume ***A New Resonance* 8**
Residence **Strasburg PA**
Occupation **Writer/Reporter**
Collection ***The Celesta Made of Water***

Since appearing in *A New Resonance* 8 I've published a small collection of 30 haiku *The Celesta Made of Water*, which can be found on the *Bones* website, and another collection forthcoming. I've also had haiku appear in Modern Haiku Press's *Haiku 2014*, *Haiku 2015* and *Haiku 2016*. I was also honored to have one of my haiku selected as the favorite haiku of issue 47.1 of *Modern Haiku*. Recently, I helped launch a weekly haiku feature at the newspaper I work for and Lancaster County readers are filling my inbox with their poems! Working on my little haiku e-book for *Bones* was such a fun experience and I hope to do more things like that in the future. My wife did all the art for that so that was a really cool thing to be able to do. I've also had some other poems and stories appear in journals such as *Faded Out, Occulum, Fluland* and elsewhere. You can find all these by searching the internet.

* poem about disappointment but it's only the word sea
  is/let March 6, 2017

in their dark glass tank
the lobsters orbiting
the sun
  Modern Haiku 47.1

a blue wind
erasing the Latin names
of ferns
  Modern Haiku 47.3

the avalanche
the sea foam and the bears
all made of mist
  A Hundred Gourds 4.3

ice ages and motel mini fridges
tumbling over the
endless mountains
  Hedgerow 24

the lightbulb moon
a brown moth rolls its wings
into cigarettes
  Modern Haiku 48.3

Name **Susan Antolin**
Volume *A New Resonance* 7
Residence **Walnut Creek CA**
Occupation **Writer / Editor**
Collection *Artichoke Season*

Over the past decade, I have served in various positions in the haiku community, including editor of the print newsletter, *Ripples*, for the Haiku Society of America; editor of the print newsletter for the Haiku Poets of Northern California; President of the Haiku Poets of Northern California; and the job I love most, editor of *Acorn: a Journal of Contemporary Haiku*. I have also served as a judge for many years of the Richmond Writes poetry contest for students in Richmond, California and occasionally give haiku workshops for children and adults in the Bay Area. My collection of haiku and tanka, *Artichoke Season*, was published in 2009. I almost never miss a meeting of the Haiku Poets of Northern California and have become a regular/fanatical attendee of the Haiku North America conferences. More than 25 years ago, I lived for three years in Japan, where I met my husband, Ed. Now that we've mostly raised our three children (the youngest will leave for college this year), we hope to resume travelling. In the meantime, we spend our free time hiking in the foothills of Mt. Diablo with our dogs, exploring local restaurants, and browsing in the few remaining local bookstores.

curriculum vitae
the years
that went missing
Close to the Wind

summer clouds
I pull the rope ladder up
behind me
Modern Haiku 45.1

a light snowfall without forming opinions
Full of Moonlight

assigning my pain a number of autumn clouds
Frogpond 37.1

night sky
one of those stars might be
the reset button
Modern Haiku 46.2

inauguration day
newsprint darkens
my fingers
Mariposa 36

Name **Annie Bachini**
Volume ***A New Resonance* 1**
Residence **London, England**
Occupation **Retired**
Collection ***The River's Edge***

I received a second prize in the Kusamakura Haiku Contest 2014 and, alongside other anthologies, was pleased to be included in *Haiku in English: The First Hundred Years* in 2013. I was honoured to represent Britain at the Haiku International Association's 20th anniversary symposium in 2009. Whilst a member of the British Haiku Society I served as president (2007 – 2009); edited one surreal issue and subsequent sections of *Blithe Spirit* in 2003, and edited the newletter 1995 – 1997. Since leaving the British Haiku Society in 2009 I have been training and performing, primarily in clown. I also teach a haiku short course.

cat in the garden untangling twilight
Kusamakura Haiku Contest 2014 2nd Prize

tight buds
on the Japanese anemone
people I used to know
Presence 53

no crackle
in the wet leaves
the movement of clouds
Notes from the Gean 2011

not having dogs
we talk about
our shopping trolleys
Presence 58

toothache
briefly absorbed
by the full moon
Presence 51

learning about
quantitative easing
the cat and the fiddle
Presence 57

Name **Deb Baker**
Volume ***A New Resonance* 4**
Residence **Concord NH**
Occupation **Ass't. Director of Libraries**

I'm a writer and insatiable reader. I blog at bookconscious and The Nocturnal Librarian, and tweet as @bookconscious and @NoctLibrarian. I am a late-night reference librarian at Rivier University. My writing is often inspired by the nine states where I've lived, my autodidactic family, and social justice issues. My poems and essays have appeared in journals on three continents. My awards and other honors include being featured in *A New Resonance 4: Emerging Voices in English-Language Haiku* (Red Moon Press, 2005); and an Honorable Mention in the Kaji Aso Studio International Haiku Contest (2006).

waking up
before the plow
snow silence
bottle rockets 11

warm afternoon
my daughter's eyes close
as I read
The Heron's Nest VI:11

after mowing
the cold cucumber
on my tongue
bottle rockets 10

thick heat
suddenly dragonflies
above the swings
Acorn 12

candlelight
your voice moves
into shadow
Frogpond 27.3

dark house —
in the microwave
my forgotten mug
unpublished

Name **Stewart Baker**
Volume *A New Resonance* 9
Residence **Dallas OR**
Occupation **Academic Librarian**

Even though I now mostly write and publish fiction, I still consider myself a haikuist. Haiku is more than just poetry to me — it represents a greater awareness of small things in the world around us (and in imagined worlds, too). Even if I'm not submitting (or even writing down) haiku as much any more, I appreciate that skill as a general benefit. More pragmatically, it's proved very useful to me as I move forward with a science fiction career, helping me to focus on what's really important in a story or to find an arresting story title. This has served me well — I've won or been shortlisted for several fiction contests and awards since appearing in *A New Resonance* 9. I've also been successful at longer-form poetry, with my poem "The Fragmented Poet Files a Police Report" taking the first place (long form) prize in the Science Fiction Poetry Association's 2017 poetry contest. I also stay involved with haiku through my role as web editor of *The Heron's Nest*, setting each issue and taking care of routine web maintenance tasks, and writing the occasional essay about haiku that are selected for the editors' choice awards.

tide pool stars
the universe expanding
in his daughter's eyes
Frogpond 38.3

I learn to tell
cherries from plums . . .
late bloomer
Modern Haiku 46.3

wave function collapse —
the last cherry blossom lands
as she says I do
ARC Centre of Excellence for Engineered Quantum Systems October 2015

standing stones
the arc of the sun's shadow
on an empty grave
Chrysanthemum 18

mud pies
I tell my son about
privilege
A Hundred Gourds 4.4

Name **Francine Banwarth**
Volume ***A New Resonance* 5**
Residence **Dubuque IA**
Occupation **Freelance Proofreader**
Collection ***The Haiku Life***

After the honor of appearing in *A New Resonance* 5, I continued to study and workshop haiku and its related forms with groups in Dubuque and Mineral Point, Wisconsin. I served as second vice president of the Haiku Society of America for three years and on the board of *Modern Haiku* for four years. In 2012 I was named editor of the HSA's journal, *Frogpond*, and served in that capacity through 2015. Editing the journal helped expand my understanding of haiku and influenced my writing practice. In 2017, Modern Haiku Press published *The Haiku Life*, coauthored with *Frogpond* associate editor, Michele Root-Bernstein. Through these years I've learned that the art of haiku has continued to evolve and enrich our lives, and I am grateful for all of the mentors, editors, judges, and anthologists who believe in our work.

off to on I disappear into the visible
Frogpond 39.1; Museum of Haiku Literature Award

the carving knife
out of its sheath
winter darkness
The Heron's Nest XVII:1

fallen leaves me with my grudges
Modern Haiku 46.1

fireflies . . .
someone leaving
someone coming home
The Heron's Nest XVIII:3

autumn fog . . .
the river knows
the way
Shiki Kukai 2009 1st Place

disorderly conduct the wildflower wind
Frogpond 43

Name	Colin Barber
Volume	*A New Resonance* 5
Residence	Marion AR
Occupation	MRI Technologist
Collection	*The Devil Is a Child*

I am an artist who discovered a love for haiku in 2004. I'm married with 3 children and work at a hospital in Memphis, Tennessee. My haiku honors include being featured in *A New Resonance 5: Emerging Voices in English-Language Haiku* (Red Moon Press, 2007); first place finishes in The Shiki Monthly Kukai (May 2008) and The Shiki Monthly Kukai (August 2009); and prizes in the Gerald Brady Senryu Awards (2007), Modern Haiku Haiku Award (2008), and Modern Haiku Senryu Award (2008).

one more game
of shirts vs. skins
summer dusk
The Heron's Nest VIII:2

morning chill —
I move to her side
of the argument
Modern Haiku 38.3

honeymoon over my suntan peels
Frogpond 30.1

spring fever the thermometer's long red line
Chrysanthemum 1

another first date . . .
I fail again
to be myself
Shiki Kukai September 2006

snow flurries
my haiku money
in the vending machine
unpublished

Name Janelle Barrera
Volume *A New Resonance* 5
Residence Key West FL
Occupation Retired Teacher

The person who introduced haiku to me was Lee Gurga. I used to argue with him about haiku content and rules. Yes, completely ignorant, and innocent of the fact, I was! He knew what he knew and tolerated what I didn't know. I have judged quite a few haiku contests since then to prove that I listened and learned eventually. When we held the Robert Frost Poetry Festival in Key West for several springs, I was able to get Lee, Charlie Trumbull and Barry George to present haiku workshops. They were favorites of the poetry writers. After Lee gave up his Key Ku project in Solaris Hill, I took over as editor until the newspaper supplement folded. Rather than say what I have accomplished, not that much truthfully, I would like to say how being included by Jim Kacian in *A New Resonance* was very special for me. Also, the following people: John Stevenson, Peggy Lyles, Francine Banwarth, Robert Epstein, Ion Codrescu, and Scott Mason, have in some way inspired and encouraged me to practice the art of haiku.

mockingbirds hush
leaving me a day to pass
until evening song
Something Out of Nothing

chipmunks, a bird or two —
this winter park
without you
Gazing at Flowers

wide open
the roses we leave
on the motel dresser
Spiess Haiku Contest 2008

our cab ride
one love song long . . .
spring moon
The Heron's Nest 2010

ashes of roses
what once was our secret
now just mine
The Heron's Nest 2009

stone cold ground —
the year that took my love
also gone
SP Quill 2008

Name **Jack Barry**
Volume *A New Resonance 3*
Residence **Ashfield MA**
Occupation **Housepainter/Carpenter**
Collections *After the Eclipse*
All Nite Rain
Swamp Candles
The Winter Garden

It's been twenty years since Mr. Robert Spiess finally, finally said yes to a couple of my poems. Since then, haiku has developed from just a nice little art form into one of the essential tools in my education as a human being. More than ever I see this planet as a vast school, where the best we can do is to learn a) what we are and b) how that being fits in to the world around it. These little poems have turned out to be ideally suited for this process; rather than being clever or didactic or even just pretty, at their best haiku are written records of those fleeting moments of comprehension, when the apparently differentiated material world is suddenly revealed as an intricate, shimmering web of relationships. I go through long spells now when I am so absorbed in this network it doesn't even occur to me to find words to describe my experience. Or, perhaps, I am just too dull-witted. That being said, years of habit have left their mark, and I am still never without pen and paper, always ready for that next notable moment, because, as we all know: you're only as good as your last haiku.

white caps
one cliff swallows sails
away from the rest
The Winter Garden

the whole line of ducks
pops over a wave
already gone
The Winter Garden

4 AM
meditation
a
plume
of
woodsmoke
rises
to
the
moon
The Winter Garden

following the wrack line
the one legged gull's
perfect print
The Winter Garden

funeral procession
the solitary oak
still holds its leaves
dedicated to the memory
of Jane Wildfong
unpublished

Name Robert Bauer
Volume *A New Resonance* 5
Born 2 July 1953
Died 2 December 2012

gust front
the lineman strips a wire
with his teeth
A New Resonance 5

light snow
I add slaked lime
to the mortar
A New Resonance 5

winter sunset
a rusted wedge
stuck in oak
A New Resonance 5

a mud wasps crawls
out of the wind chime —
summer's end
A New Resonance 5

autumn sunrise
the scent of sage lingers
in the prayer lodge
A New Resonance 5

first snow
the gypsy slips some beans
into her mojo
A New Resonance 5

Name: Roberta Beary
Volume: *A New Resonance 2*
Residence: Westport, Ireland
Occupation: Writer
Collections: *Nothing Left to Say*
The Unworn Necklace
Deflection

I write haiku to speak for the disenfranchised, to let them know they are not alone. Human rights, especially those affecting the young LGBTQ global community, are reflected in my haiku. The lack of recognition of women haiku poets is a personal one for me, which I am helping to redress as co-editor of an anthology of haiku by women. As Roving Ambassador for The Haiku Foundation I have met haiku poets, done readings, and conducted workshops in Singapore, Australia, New Zealand, Sweden, Denmark, Netherlands, and Ireland. My haibun collection, *Deflection* (Accents Publishing, 2015) won an HSA Book Award and was a finalist for Eric Hoffer Book Awards and a Touchstone Award HM. I co-curated the exhibit *Haiku Quilts* which featured haiku by Haiku Ireland poets and quilts by Octagon Quilters of Westport, Ireland for the 2017 Westport Arts Festival. Haiku Quilts went on to be exhibited at public libraries in Ireland. My retirement from the active practice of law has allowed me to focus my time on spreading the haiku word around the world. In preparation for my travels I donated my haiku manuscripts, book collections, and memorabilia to The Haiku Foundation Archives. I believe this type of legacy is important for the future of global haiku.

library fly
at rest on
hamlet's soliloquy
26th Ito-en Haiku Contest
Honorable Mention

abortion day
a shadow flutters
the fish tank
Rattle 47
Pushcart Prize Nominee

bicurious the moon within the moon
Presence 53

sea breeze
a sandpiper
rearranges itself
28th Ito-en Haiku Contest

born this way ...
the orientation
of winter stars
Acorn 35

just friends —
a taste of summer
in her kiss
European Haiku Kukai 2013
Third Place

Name: Brad Bennett
Volume: *A New Resonance* 9
Residence: Arlington MA
Occupation: Teacher
Collection: *a drop of pond*

Modern Haiku 47.1 spotlighted my work in winter 2016. I've had poems included in the *Red Moon Anthologies* of 2015 and 2016. I've placed in a few haiku contests, and one of my poems was shortlisted for The Haiku Foundation's Touchstone Award for Individual Poems for 2016. Another one of my poems was voted *Shamrock Haiku Journal* Readers' Choice Awards 2016 Best Haiku. My first book-length collection of haiku, *a drop of pond*, was published by Red Moon Press in July 2016. It was awarded a Touchstone Distinguished Book Award by The Haiku Foundation. I have given readings at the Haiku Gathering at Wild Graces in Deerfield, New Hampshire, a meeting of the Haiku Poets' Society of Western Massachusetts, poetry classes at the Boston Conservatory at Berklee, and Haiku North America 2017 in Santa Fe, New Mexico. My article "Children's Haiku Books: An Annotated Bibliography," appeared in *Modern Haiku* 46.3. In my role as co-chair of The Haiku Foundation's Education Resources Committee, I have helped to organize a blog feature called "Teaching Stories." During the spring of 2017, I co-judged the Nicholas Virgilio Memorial Haiku and Senryu Competition. I live with my wonderful partner and first reader, Barbara Schwartz, and teach at a progressive independent school in Cambridge, Massachusetts. I continue to enjoy teaching haiku to third and fourth grade students in my class and to other kids during an afterschool poetry club.

winter sun
a crow gives in
to the wind
Presence 55

snowy winter
less down
to the see saw
Porad Award 2015
Honorable Mention

Grand Canyon
neither of us mentions
the silence
Spiess Haiku Competition 2016
Honorable Mention

news of a shooting . . .
the leaves that fall faster
than the others
Modern Haiku 47.1

after the fighter
a goldfinch recaptures
the sky
Shamrock 35
Readers' Choice Awards 2016
Best Haiku

late August
fewer seconds between
lightning and thunder
Modern Haiku 46.2

Name **Johan Bergstad**
Volume ***A New Resonance* 10**
Residence **Hedemora, Sweden**
Occupation **Psychologist/Writer**

I have written haiku since 2002 and my poetry has appeared in *Acorn, Blåeld, Fri Haiku, Frogpond, Modern Haiku, The Heron's Nest* and *White Lotus*. I've also been included in several anthologies, such as *Nest Feathers: Selected Haiku from the First 15 Years of The Heron's Nest* (2015); *dust of summers: The Red Moon Anthology of English–Language Haiku* (2008); *Silently the Morning Breaks: Ten Swedish Haiku Poets* (Östasieninstitutet, 2008); *Snowdrops: Eleven Swedish Haiku Poets* (Bokverket, 2009); *Haiku of Sweden* (The Haiku Foundation, 2016); *Kamesan's World Haiku Anthology on War, Violence and Human Rights Violation* (CreateSpace, 2013); and *Through the leaves* (Svenska Haiku Sällskapet, 2017). In 2017 a Swedish artist, Ania Witwitzka, interpreted some 40 of my haiku in fine art form and we held an exhibition, "A ship leaves," together. I am also a keen photographer and in 2008 my photo collage won *The Heron's Nest* illustration contest. I live in the village in Dalarna, Sweden, with my wife and four children. We like to travel and have spent extended time in India, Vietnam, Thailand, Australia and New Zealand. I am the founder of Mindfulness Academy Scandinavia, and have written two books about mindfulness as well as recorded several apps. I've also written books for children, and am working on a novel for teens. I give talks to companies and organizations about mindfulness, focus and compassion trainings.

new temple
all tourists gather
in the wi-fi zone
<small>unpublished</small>

pedestrian crossing
I stop for
the full moon
<small>unpublished</small>

quiet section
I regret
the carrot
<small>*Through the leaves*</small>

cancer diagnosis
the child's first
"I love you"
<small>*Through the leaves*</small>

a ship leaves
some of the sea
is rain
<small>*Modern Haiku* 39.3</small>

full moon night
all that is
and isn't
<small>*Frogpond* 32.1</small>

Name **Harsangeet Kaur Bhullar**
Volume ***A New Resonance* 1**
Residence **Newport Wales**
Occupation **Founder, WISE KIDS**

A lot has happened since *A New Resonance Volume 1* was published almost 20 years ago. In 2002, my husband and I moved our young family (3 children) from Singapore back to the UK. In the immediate years afterwards, I continued to write haiku albeit much less frequently, as the demands of work and a young family made it more difficult. Whilst I haven't been an active contributor for a while, I have, over the years, had some collaborations with haiku friends — for example, Paul Mena — and I hosted WINTER 2006 Haiku, Tanka, Haiga, Haibun and Senyru blogs. I also participated in autumn and summer seasonal blogs. I have a haiku website I update sporadically. Over the years, my haiku have appeared in a number of publications including *Chaba*, *Frogpond*, and *Woodnotes*. Apart from *A New Resonance*, my haiku have also appeared in *Haikü Sans Frontières*, an anthology edited by Andre Duhaime, and *Haiku Poetry Ancient and Modern*, an anthology compiled by Jackie Hardy and published by MQ publications in 2002. Life continues to move apace! My children are all grown up now, and whilst work does keep me busy, I continue to read and write haiku and learn. I would love to reconnect with friends old and new in the haiku community again!

orchid in half blossom —
   on its stem
      a praying mantis . . .
Frogpond 19.2

    in the hat
    silver pennies
    covered in drizzle
chaba

      monsoon rain —
      the finger-painted poster
      dripping. . . .
Shiki Internet Salon

deepening twilight
   the stranger in front
     walks faster . . .
Woodnotes 31

distant roll of thunder —
the empty cab light
fading into darkness
Beyond Spiritual Borders

dusk —
the dog walker
looks the other way
unpublished

Name **Johannes S. H. Bjërg**
Volume ***A New Resonance* 8**
Residence **Höjby Denmark**
Occupation **Writer / Artist**
Collections ***Penguins / Pingviner***
rainflames

I am a Dane who writes in Danish and English simultaneously and mainly haiku and haiku related forms. 1 of 3 of the editors of *Bones: Journal for contemporary haiku*, and sole editor of *the other bunny — for the other kind of haibun* and *One Link Chain*, a blog for solo linked verse and haiku sequences. I have published several books.

failing eternally a discussion of the ratio between dead poets and trees

(winter kigo)
the silence
of apples

from the haibun "sunset outside"

97th sneeze
how to calibrate
a missing horizon

January
by moving a chair
the world changes

days of glass
the fish inside you
turns opaque

without its sound how long will your song be?

Name: Meik Blöttenberger
Volume: *A New Resonance* 10
Residence: Hanover PA
Occupation: Non-Profit Coordinator

Since appearing in *A New Resonance* 10, my haiku have been awarded a first place in The Montenegrin Haiku Contest, a third place in Our Little Iris Haiku Contest, and two honorable mentions. I've also had three haiku appear in Scott Mason's *The Wonder Code: Discover the Way of Haiku and See the World with New Eyes*. The haiku community has been very welcoming to me and I'm pleased to be a part of it. I was born in Baltimore to German immigrant parents. I am currently living in Hanover, Pennsylvania and in a decade will be retiring to the high desert of Arizona. My other passions include photography and traveling.

staring match
sheep on the other side
of a split rail fence

    Montenegrin Haiku Contest 2017
    First Prize

first light
about to touch
butterfly eggs

    Kaji Aso Haiku Contest 2017
    Honorable Mention

saving a wasp
in the birdbath
this man I've become

    Write Like Issa

fleeing war . . .
in a child's fist,
chickpeas

    Our Little Iris Haiku Contest 2017
    Third Prize

cherry blossom breeze
the schnauzer runs
without a leash

    Vancouver Cherry Blossom Festival 2017
    USA Sakura Award

blue-green dragonfly
racing against its shadow
how slow the earth spins

    Tokutomi Haiku Contest 2016
    Honorable Mention

Name **Mark E. Brager**
Volume *A New Resonance* 10
Residence **Columbia MD**
Occupation **Public Affairs Executive**

Still trying to fill the spaces between words . . .

tsunami
somewhere
a butterfly
IAFOR Contest 2018

mountain summit
—
back
bent by the weight
of
stars
Ito-en Oi Ocha Haiku Contest 2018

swimming upstream
the Jesus fish
Bones 14

old pond
deep in my pocket
a wishing stone
The Heron's Nest XX:1

without
  you . . .
losing
  hold
of
  the rain
Modern Haiku 49.1

her scars
deeper than bone . . .
winter solstice
tinywords December 21, 2017

Name **Alan Bridges**
Volume *A New Resonance 7*
Residence **Littleton MA**
Occupation **Oil/Natural Gas Producer**
Collection *in a flash*

I was introduced to haiku by John Stevenson in 2008. In 2017 I was voted Poet of the Year (2016) by the readers of *The Heron's Nest*. Also in 2017 I was awarded first place in the Robert Spiess Memorial Haiku Competition and was named a winner of the Snapshot Press eChapbook annual competition for *in a flash*, which will be published in the spring, 2018. I am grateful for the friendships, peace and mindfulness that the haiku community has afforded me. In addition to owning a small independent oil and natural gas production company, I work three jobs at a hospital, which provide haiku inspiration as does the view of the Sudbury River. I have always enjoyed nature and being outside, and haiku provides me a way to share what I see and feel. I enjoy skiing, fishing and an occasional horseback ride. One of my favorite haiku poets is Nicholas A. Virgilio. My girls Holly and Emma are a source of joy in the world beyond poetry.

an old song pours
from a Navajo toehold
canyon wren

> Spiess Memorial Contest 2017
> First Place

gale-force wind
a bird's nest becomes
what it was

> IHS International Contest 2012
> First Place

wheat equidistant from each ocean

> *The Heron's Nest* XV:3

retelling the story animal bones

> Porad Award 2015
> First Place

petroglyph
the wear on the rock
where he stood

> *Hedgerow* 122

full flower moon
a soft-shelled crab
emerges from itself

> Kaji Aso Contest 2015
> First Place

Name	Helen Buckingham
Volume	*A New Resonance* 5
Residence	Wells, Somerset, UK
Occupation	Writer
Collections	*water on the moon*
	mirrormoon
	Armadillo Basket
	sanguinella

My work appears regularly in journals such as *Frogpond, The Heron's Nest, is/let, Mayfly, Modern Haiku* & *Presence*. Anthology publications include several in the *Red Moon* series, and *Haiku in English: The First Hundred Years* (Norton, 2013). My work has been placed and mentioned in awards including: The Basho Festival, Betty Drevniok, British Haiku Society: James W. Hackett, Haiku Dreaming Australia, European Haiku, Genkissu, Golden Haiku, HIA, Ito En Oi O-cha, Kusamakura, Mainichi, Martin Lucas, Setouchi Matsuyama, Snapshot Calendar, Suruga-Baika, Touchstone, Vancouver Haiku Invitational, and With Words. I was born in South London, 1960, and moved to the southwest of England in my late teens. I came to writing poetry in my early twenties, largely as a result of illness (childhood meningitis had left its mark in a number of ways). It wasn't until my thirties that I discovered haiku and it proved to be life-changing, combining my love of poetry with a way of helping me access the moment, something my body had always gone to great lengths to avoid. Owing to a groundbreaking series of operations, I am finally receiving a good deal of relief from the nerve damage that has been with me for so long. Haiku, nonetheless, remains central to my life.

    day one of the fast —
    the image of Ganesha
    stuck to my fridge
        Frogpond 31.3

    wi-fi beach
    raising a shell
    to each ear
        Mayfly 50

that point of white before christ muscles in
   Roadrunner 10.3

at seven we are replicants
   Bones 2

    snow
    its own
    cathedral
      The Heron's Nest XIX:1

    daybreak
    blackdog
    pixelating
      NOON 10

Name **Allan Burns**
Volume *A New Resonance* 6
Residence Fort Collins CO
Occupation Editor
Collections *distant virga*
thronging cranes
Earthlings
To Kyoto

I edited the *Montage* series, which originally appeared on The Haiku Foundation website and was later collected in book form. I also wrote and edited the anthology *Where the River Goes: The Nature Tradition in English-Language Haiku* (Snapshot Press, 2013) and co-edited *Haiku in English: The First Hundred Years* (W.W. Norton, 2013). In addition, I edited two online annuals of nature haiku, titled *Muttering Thunder,* with artwork by Ron Moss. My collection *distant virga* was published by Red Moon Press in 2011. I've also published three electronic chapbooks: *thronging cranes, Earthlings,* and *To Kyoto*. My work has won a number of Touchstone and Merit Book awards.

a willow reveals
the underground stream . . .
Dharma Day
Modern Haiku 41.1

ice floes . . .
the wren's many poses
on the reed
Acorn 30

the dog's path
less straight
than the path
South by Southeast 18.1

the way open
in all directions
wild snapdragons
Frogpond 38.3

lakeside stillness —
the cormorant's flight
starts time again
Modern Haiku 42.1

the caged chimpanzee
injected with hepatitis
signs hello
bottle rockets 28

Name Sondra Byrnes
Volume *A New Resonance* 10
Residence Santa Fe NM
Occupation Retired Attorney

Haiku is part of my every day. In 2015, I started a haiku group with Charlie Trumbull here in Santa Fe. After two years together as a group, we published *Open Spaces*, a chapbook of members' haiku. I was elected Secretary of the Haiku Society of America for the year 2016. After two years of planning, the Haiku North America 2017 conference was held in Santa Fe; I was on the small Organizing Committee. By all accounts, it was a great success. Writing haiku, my Zen practice and *chanoyu* (tea ceremony) are all of a piece: paying attention.

dusk
the soft light
of waiting
Frogpond 40.3

that favorite song
a raven catches
the thermal
Sonic Boom 9

snail drool—
just trying to make
conversation
Modern Haiku 48.3

summer night
as suddenly as the noise
the silence
Acorn 39

one garden
overwrites another
light snow
Golden Triangle Contest 2017
Runner-Up

backing into a memory
by mistake
lilacs
Prune Juice 22

Name: Yvonne Cabalona
Volume: *A New Resonance 3*
Residence: Modesto CA
Occupation: Retired
Collection: *Down the Mermaid's Back*

Since retiring, my beading muse has supplanted my haiku muse. Every once in a while, though, a visual will strike me and I find I am reaching for something to write on. Since *Echoes* 1 was published, I had a modest little book of haiku, "Down the Mermaid's Back", published in 2010 through cafe' nietzsche press. It was just in time, too. My mother passed away the following year. For the majority of the time, I have been a member of the Central Valley Haiku Club which is based in Sacramento, CA. For 16 years we held a haibun contest named for a founding member of the club, Jerry Kilbride. Our group also held yearly readings at the Gekkeikan Sake Factory in Folsom, CA during the October Arts and Humanities Month. Poetry, then *sake* . . . some attendees found it a great combination! Recently, after reading a couple of inspiring books, *They Gave Us Life* edited by Robert Epstein, and *The Wonder Code* by Scott Mason, I found myself drawn to this art form once again and I began writing. I was rewarded by having two poems selected for upcoming issues of *bottle rockets*. It shows me no matter how far away I stray from it, I still look at the world through haiku eyes.

last day of school
lessons clapped
from the erasers
The Heron's Nest 2008

such stillness
I absorb the sound
of creaking bamboo
The Heron's Nest 2009

more rain
I know I know I squawk back
to a jay
The Heron's Nest 2010

rope swing
a kid launches himself straight
into summer
Mariposa 25

collectibles store
my mixed feelings about
the mammy doll
bottle rockets 31

turtle . . .
the times
I've withdrawn
bottle rockets 32

Name **David Caruso**
Volume *A New Resonance* 8
Residence **Haddonfield NJ**
Occupation **HS English Teacher**

A few years ago, I decided to make a career change and become a high school English teacher. My experience with the haiku community greatly influenced my decision. While I don't teach haiku every day, I do spend my professional days teaching teenagers language arts. As of late, I spend more time helping others write poetry as opposed to writing poems myself. However, while I haven't been published lately, I still feel a strong connection to the haiku community.

        father's things
        digging in the deepest chests
        for i love you
            bottle rockets 30

there's no name
for everything i had . . .
the hurricane's name
   Modern Haiku 45.1

        where teeth once were . . .
        the prisoner's blade
        beneath his pillow
            VerseWrights

all them dishes
in the kitchen SINK SINK
SINK TITANIC
   bottle rockets 30

        road atlas
        the plans we made
        in thin, blue ink
            HaikuNow! 2013

Name Yu Chang
Volume *A New Resonance* 1
Residence Schenectady NY
Occupation Retired College Professor
Collections *seeds*
Small Things Make Me Laugh

I was lucky to be in the first issue of A New Resonance in 1999, and since then some of my poems have found their way into print, including, the Museum of Haiku Literature, The Harold G. Henderson Contest winner, *Acorn, Frogpond, Modern Haiku, The Heron's Nest*, and the *Red Moon Anthologies*. The Route 9 Haiku Group (with Ion Codrescu, Hilary Tann, John Stevenson, Tom Clausen) is in its 17th year of producing the biannual anthology, *Upstate Dim Sum*, and we have done readings at various haiku conferences and venues such as at Cornell's Mann Library. I had the good fortune to give a reading/workshop at Haiku Circle in 2017 ("Renku Scent in Haiku Arrangement" haikucircle.com). A collection of my poems, *Seeds*, was published in 2009 by Red Moon Press, and another collection, *Small Things Make Me Laugh*, was published by Free Food Press in 2016. Since my retirement from Union College in 2014, I have been enjoying my daily walk in Schenectady's Central Park, and talking to the trees. Haiku has become a way of life.

water lilies
our days
in the sun
The Heron's Nest XVIII:4

mating season
I am
all ears
The Heron's Nest XV:3

Valentine's Day —
thawing a wild salmon
from the supermarket
The Heron's Nest XIV:2

writing cursive
my unspoken fear
of dancing
The Heron's Nest XV:2

lingering goodbye
we all
grew a little
Upstate Dim Sum 2017/II

Central Park
a veteran's war story
still raw
Modern Haiku 48.1

Name **Joyce Clement**
Volume *A New Resonance 7*
Residence **Bristol CT**
Occupation **Sales & Marketing Manager**
Collection ***Beyond My View***

My haiku have been published in a variety of online and print journals and anthologies. I was a featured poet in *A New Resonance* 7: Emerging Voices in English-Language Haiku (Red Moon Press), and my book *Beyond My View* received a Haiku Society of America's Merit Book Award. I was also a 2014 Haiku Foundation Touchstone Award winner. Since 2011, I have served as a director of The Haiku Circle, an annual gathering of haiku poets held each June in Northfield, MA. I also recently served as co-editor of The Haiku Society of America's international journal *Frogpond*. Born & raised in upstate New York, I have lived & worked in central Connecticut for the last 30 years.

night time
in the hospice aquarium
the pulse of fish gills
The Heron's Nest XVI:2

age 88
all the *whatchamacallits*
in the spring wind
The Heron's Nest XIII:2

tea steam evaporating a dream of snow monkeys
Frogpond 37.3

dry winter days
again closing the drawer
opening by itself
Evening Stillness

B positive
even my blood type
full of advice
Modern Haiku 45.3

all the way to the vanishing point cicada
Frogpond 36.3

Name Kirsten Cliff
Volume *A New Resonance* 8
Residence Hamilton New Zealand
Occupation Librarian
Collection *thinking of you*

Since *ANR8*, I released my first e-chapbook on Valentine's Day 2014, and completed a manuscript of haiku and tanka about my experiences of going through treatment for leukaemia, which has never been published. However, by the end of that year, I mostly let go of my involvement with the haiku community due to severe storm damage to my home whilst being in the process of starting my own business. Now that I'm settled in a new home and town, and in a new job that reflects my recent two years of fulltime study, I hope to bring haiku to the students in my school. My goal would be to get a group of students to enter the Junior Haiku Section of the New Zealand Poetry Society International Poetry Competition, which I had the pleasure of judging in 2013.

spring rains the colours mixing within me
A Hundred Gourds 3.3

cry of a peacock
I wake up fully clothed
in my pain
Pulse 15 August 2014

turning hawk
how quickly these tears
dry in the breeze
Kokado 20

speckled egg
the sunlight
on my thoughts
The Heron's Nest XVI:1

stagnant water
he tells me it's okay
to give up
Presence 49

his paintbrush
against the water jar
longest night
Sharpening the Green Pencil 2014

Name **Glenn C. Coats**
Volume *A New Resonance* 3
Residence **Carolina Shores NC**
Occupation **Retired Reading Teacher**
Collections *Snow on the Lake*
Beyond the Muted Trees
waking and dream

In the 1990s I began to integrate ideas from William J. Higginson's *Haiku Handbook* into my work as a guest author. Those experiences led me to attempting my own haiku, then to reading everything that I could find. I should have started with the latter. I served as a haibun editor at *Haibun Today* for five years where I learned much from my colleagues. My haiku have received first prize in the following awards: The Winter Moon Awards for Haiku 2009, The North Carolina Poetry Society 2010, Peggy Willis Lyles Haiku Awards 2017. Two collections of haibun (*Snow on the Lake, Beyond the Muted Trees*) were published by Pineola Press. A third collection (*waking and dream*) was published by Red Moon Press in 2017. I live with my wife Joan in coastal North Carolina where we enjoy the waterways, birds, and spending time with family and friends. Music is an important part of my life, and I play guitar with friends in a band called Chicken Bog.

winter shadows
I try to tell my mother
who I am
The Haiku Calendar 2017

rippled water
I see mother's cursive
in mine
The Heron's Nest XIX:2

winter cabin
the guitar wrapped
in a blanket
Acorn 37

barred owl
father answers
with silence
Frogpond 39.3

river dark
a taste of snow
on her lips
Chrysanthemum 20

burnt coffee
the taste of nothing
left to say
Frogpond 40.1

Name　Kathy Lippard Cobb
Volume　*A New Resonance* 3
Residence　Bradenton FL
Occupation　Graphic Designer

I reside (with my cats) in Bradenton, Florida and am a recent graduate from Manatee Community College (graphic design). I have been writing haiku since 2000. My haiku have been published worldwide, and may be found in *American Tanka, Modern Haiku, Presence, Ribbons*, and various anthologies. My awards include First place in the Harold G. Henderson Haiku Competition 2001; the British Haiku Society/James W. Hackett International Haiku Award 2001; and the Haiku Presence Award 2001; second place in the Betty Drevniok Award 2001; the *Yellow Moon* Literary Competition 2002; third place in the International Kusamakura Haiku Contest 2002; many other honorable mentions, commendeds, and highly commendeds.

broken easel —
the front yard blue
with wildflowers
    Henderson Contest 2001
    First Prize

scattering at sea . . .
the great blue heron
glides through him
    Hackett Contest 2002
    First Prize

tiny headstone —
a pinwheel turns
the wind
    Haiku Presence Competition 2002
    Second Prize

a catfish twitches
at the end of the line —
fading daylight
    Acorn 10

gangsta rap echoes
through the bayou . . .
moonlight mist
    Presence 39

veterans day parade —
the homeless man stands
on a different corner
    Frogpond 25.1

Name **Pamela Connor**
Volume *A New Resonance* 1
Residence **Luzerne PA**
Occupation **Gallery Owner**

No update.

> heat wave . . .
> the gravedigger lays his lunch
> on white marble
> > unpublished

spring cleaning
an unmarked box
filled with mother's smell
> unpublished

> morning sunshine . . .
> the jingle of coins
> in my pocket
> > unpublished

my simple uncle
no wisdom lines
on his old face
> *Modern Haiku* 26.1

> snow angels
> almost invisible
> under new snow
> > unpublished

wrapping myself
into my father's shirt —
favorite shade of blue
> unpublished

Name Susan Constable
Volume *A New Resonance* 6
Residence Parksville BC
Occupation Retired

After several years of composing haiku and haiga, I began writing tanka and, from 2012 to 2016, was the tanka editor for the online journal *A Hundred Gourds*. I've enjoyed acting as a judge for three haiku and/or tanka contests and co-editing two anthologies. For ten years, I was a member on Jane Reichhold's *AHA Poetry Forum* and am now extremely active on *Inkstone*, AHA's successor. I've not yet got around to publishing a collection of my work in book form and have only entered (and placed) in a few contests. To balance my hours of reading and writing, I enjoy physical activity in the form of strength training and cycling. Mild weather on the West Coast permits outdoor activities all year round and the Seabeck Haiku Getaway every autumn kickstarts my muse for the winter. I began 2017 by writing 5 haiku and 5 tanka every day for 150 days . . . and I'm still working on revisions!

Mother's Day
most of our verbs
in past tense
Modern Haiku 42.3

silence
where the river ran
this bed of stones
Acorn 36

knife cold swimming into blue bones
Modern Haiku 44.1

three-quarter moon
I want to be
the missing piece
mayfly 60

adopted —
at the river's origin
I quench my thirst
bottle rockets 34

moonlight fingering the blue of her prayers
Acorn 39

Name **Jennifer Corpe**
Volume ***A New Resonance* 7**
Residence **Norton Shores MI**
Occupation **Stay-at-Home Mom**

I won my first ever foray into a haiku competition by entering the Chicago Cicada Haiku Contest in 2007. I also placed 2nd in the White Lotus Haiku Competition that year. In 2008, I placed 3rd in the spring/summer *moonset* contest II; 2nd in the autumn/winter *moonset* contest III; 3rd in the Kusamakura Haiku Competition; was a finalist in the *Penumbra* Contest and was commended in the *White Lotus* Haiku Competition. I received an honorable mention in the Robert Spiess Memorial Haiku Awards in 2010; placed 3rd in The Anita Sadler Weiss Memorial Haiku Awards (2011); and received an honorable mention in the *Penumbra* Contest (2011). My work has been included in several books and anthologies including *seed packets: an anthology of flower haiku* (bottle rockets press, 2010); the Red Moon Anthology *Big Data* (2014); *Nest Feathers* (The Heron's Nest Press, 2015); *The Haiku Life* (Modern Haiku Press, 2017); and *The Wonder Code* (Girasole Press, 2017). I am a member of the Evergreen Haiku Study Group which meets in East Lansing, MI. I enjoy living near Lake Michigan sand dunes with my husband, son, two cats, and a pug in an octagon shaped house. All our names, coincidentally, start with "J".

April Fools' —
we gorge ourselves
on kumquats
A Hundred Gourds 1.1

fifth birthday
I count the clouds
on one hand
Acorn 28

failure to thrive . . .
the first snow falls
without sticking
Frogpond 37.3

wintry mix
the relatives
left behind
Modern Haiku 44.3

they speak
of my doppelgänger . . .
autumn's first chill
The Heron's Nest XII:4

summer solstice
a garter snake's tongue
tastes the air
The Heron's Nest XV:4

Name **Aubrie Cox**
Volume *A New Resonance* 8
Residence **Muncie IN**
Occupation **Graduate Student**
Collection *tea's aftertaste*

Academic by day, haiku poet by night, I graduated in Spring 2011 from Millikin University with a B.A. in English literature and writing. While at Millikin, where I first discovered haiku, I served as editor-in-chief for the university literary and fine arts magazine *Collage*, and senior editor for the student-run publishing company Bronze Man Books. Currently, I'm pursuing an M.A. in creative writing at Ball State University in Muncie, Indiana, as well as compiling an anthology of English-language haiku by women. My poetry has appeared in print and online journals, including *Modern Haiku, The Heron's Nest, bottle rockets, Acorn, Frogpond, tinywords, Eucalypt, Moonbathing, Sketchbook, Prune Juice, Chrysanthemum, haijinx, Mango Moons, Haiga Online,* and *Notes From the Gean*. I served as guest editor for the 2011 summer issue of the online magazine *haijinx*, and my debut chapbook *tea's aftertaste* is now available from Bronze Man Books.

roadside violet
all the places
I've yet to go
Acorn 26

warmth leaves
my teacup —
a child's cry
Frogpond 33.1

every place taken
on the finch feeder
September rain
The Heron's Nest XI:3

distant galaxies
all the things
I could've been
Modern Haiku 41.3

harvest moon
rises above the branches
tea's aftertaste
bottle rockets 23

snow day —
I cradle a bowl
of steamed rice
Mango Moons 1

Name John Crook
Volume *A New Resonance* 2
Born 8 December 1945
Died 16 April 2001

    summer solstice —
    the sun reaches a new place
    on the fridge
    Blithe Spirit 9.3

heat wave
the cat rests her head
on today's paper
Acorn 5

    stargazing
    we trip
    someone's security light
    A New Resonance 2

ancient stone circle
the flow
of a robin's song
Temps Libres

    mackerel sky —
    sheep's wool blowing
    on the barbed wire
    Modern Haiku 31.2

ebb tide —
the shell I keep reaching for
carried further away
The Heron's Nest II:8

Name **Michael Cross**
Volume *A New Resonance* 2
Residence **Seaside NJ**
Occupation **Creative Director**

No update.

        summer evening —
        the old windmill
        stirs the stars
           unpublished

forsythia —
he puts his wedding band
back on
   unpublished

        off season —
        the backstop catches
        dead leaves
           unpublished

october chill —
the irregular shapes
of green apples
   unpublished

        a long twilight —
        the click of typewriter keys
        abruptly stops
           unpublished

winter afternoon —
filling the half-flat tire
for my ex-wife
   unpublished

Name **Katherine Cudney**
Volume *A New Resonance* 4
Residence **Sonoita AZ**
Occupation **Mother / Student**

I retired from nearly 20 years of stuntwork the year my son was born and have happily spent the last decade or so up to my elbows in cheerios, spaghettiOs and laundry suds. During that time I was also gently reared in the way of haiku by one of my favorite haijin — Ferris Gilli — after submitting a few novice, misguided attempts to *The Heron's Nest* in 2002. I discovered the "it" of it during those wonderful days spent learning with her and since then I always keep a haiku butterfly net close by. Haiku and haibun have been great equalizers in my life and have propelled me to places I never would have imagined. These days, I'm working steadily toward the completion of my degree in psychology, with a minor in creative arts, at Prescott College in Tucson. Cracking the books has left me little time for much of anything else, but my notebook is full of hastily jotted notes about fleeting glimpses, quirky realizations and seemingly disconnected, keenly observed moments. There are few things as enjoyable to me as coming across a really great haiku in a book or journal and having it continue to resonate for months, even years, later. Billy Collins' "Japan", his poem about a favorite haiku, says it best for me.

sunlight
through a snail shell
and the snail
The Heron's Nest VI:3

waking to
his callused fingers
and the sound of rain
Frogpond 27.3

I am the age
my father never was
spring planting
The Heron's Nest VI:4

moonlight . . .
our newborn's tears
fill my breasts
Frogpond 27.1

letter from Iraq
a birdsong spelled
phonetically
The Heron's Nest VI:6

half-moon light
   a stone I thought
was a frog
               is
Mainichi Daily News 2004

William Cullen Jr. (*A New Resonance* 4) elected not to participate in *Echoes* 2.

Name **DeVar Dahl**
Volume ***A New Resonance* 3**
Residence **Magrath AB**
Occupation **High School Teacher**

No update.

                                the smooth place
                                where two branches rub
                                March wind
                                        unpublished

        ceramic fillings
        the woman dentist
        hums in my ear
              unpublsihed

                                news of his death
                                the cigarette smoke rises
                                straight up
                                       unpublished

        black veins
        in the dragonfly's wing —
        a hint of frost
              unpublsihed

                                pencil shavings
                                the student's tongue
                                curls and uncurls
                                        unpublsihed

        spring thaw
        the widening circles
        of a bald eagle
              unpublished

Name **Anne LB Davidson**
Volume ***A New Resonance* 4**
Residence **Saco ME**
Occupation **Writer**

No update.

        winter rain . . .
        the windshield wipers'
        same two notes
           Haiku Canada Newsletter 16.1

rain on the skylight
putting on my red sweater
to peel potatoes
   South by Southeast 6.3

        cookie crumbs
        on the car salesman's desk —
        record snowfall
           Frogpond 24.3

the small gray cloud
is now the sky . . .
first drops of rain
   Presence 19

        following the hearse . . .
        for some
        just a rainy day
           Mayfly 38

on the phone
my daughter and I
watch different sunsets
   Lilliput Review 143

Name **Ian Daw**
Volume ***A New Resonance* 4**
Residence **Lancaster UK**
Occupation **Pharmacy Technician**

No update.

    silence
    in a phone box
    drifted snow
unpublished

lightning
the crow's
hanging feet
unpublished

pruned branches joining the evening shadows
unpublished

holding the ashes that once held me
Presence 24

the shadow
in the statue's smile —
winter sun
Simply Haiku 3.3

cracked mirror
part of my face
falls through
unpublished

Name **Bill Deegan**
Volume *A New Resonance* 10
Residence **Mahwah NJ**
Occupation **Financial Professional**
Collection *a small collection*

I have been fortunate to have discovered haiku and meet many great poets over the past few years. It is truly a wonderful community of creative and kind people.

the dirty snow pile
melts a little...
New Year's Day
Acorn 39

this scoop of vanilla
just now
summer moon
Chrysanthemum 21

blueberry morning clink of the flagpole pulley
Akitsu Quarterly Winter 2017

lemon tea
the daughters remember her
hairstyles
Mayfly 63

icy morning
the metallic rattle of
the toilet roll spindle
The Heron's Nest XIX:4

Name Kristen Deming
Volume *A New Resonance 6*
Residence Bethesda MD
Occupation Retired
Collection *plum afternoon*

I was fortunate to live in Japan for over ten years as the wife of a diplomat. I made many poetry friends, was active in poetry groups, and hosted gatherings of haiku, tanka, and renku poets. In a series of happy opportunities, I spoke and wrote about haiku and was a counselor for the Haiku International Association. I helped organize two U.S.-Japan haiku conferences and co-authored a newspaper column of translations of Japanese modern haiku. I won first prize, International Division, in the Inaugural *Mainichi Daily News* haiku contest. In the U.S., I served as president of the Haiku Society of America and was a founding associate of The Haiku Foundation. I was a speaker at the Japan Information and Culture Center and a judge for National Public Radio's Cherry Blossom contest, the Virgilio contest, and others. I received the Museum of Haiku Literature award, won second place in the Henderson contest, placed third in the Spiess contest, and was runner-up in the Snapshot Press 2018 calendar. A collection of my haiku, *plum afternoon*, was published in 2017. My haiku have been included in numerous anthologies. Other than family, poetry has been the most uplifting aspect of my life. I treasure my friends in the haiku community, both here and abroad. Their poetic insights have deepened my sense of wonder, love and connection to life in all its facets.

    as if his hand
    remained in my hand —
    sun-warmed stone
        The Heron's Nest XVIII:3

alone now
no ruby slippers
to take me home
    Modern Haiku 45.2

dawn swim —
making a butterfly of water
of light
    Frogpond 36.1

new catalogue —
I order *narcissus poeticus*
just for the name
    Frogpond 36.2

    soundless rain —
    the names of the fallen
    come out of the stones
        plum afternoon

winter wake—
the room shrinks
to a candle's length
    plum afternoon

Name Bruce Detrick
Volume *A New Resonance* 2
Born 20 July 1941
Died 30 June 2001

    on chemo —
    watching my visitors
    eat the box of chocolates
        For a Moment

after surgery
and poison
the old apple tree blooms
   For a Moment

    my wheelchair by the curb
    holding a potted plant
    discharge day
        For a Moment

turning a bit wild
the garden
of the man who died
   For a Moment

    free Sunday concert
    in the slow movement
    another cane falls
        For a Moment

indian summer
sun bathing
in long pants
   For a Moment

Name Susan Diridoni
Volume *A New Resonance* 8
Residence Kensington CA
Occupation Psychotherapist

It was a pleasing announcement that two of my haiku had been chosen to appear in *Haiku in English: The First Hundred Years*. In addition, one haiku of mine appeared in *Haiku 2014* or "100 notable ku from 2013" and this was followed by another appearance in *Haiku 2015* or "100 notable ku from 2014." I have participated in many haiku readings, often at haiku meetings and occasionally as a featured reader. I am currently working on a book of my haiku — a task which has proven difficult for several years, largely because of the different styles in which I write. As a psychologist and as an investigator into creativity, I marvel at those times in life when the poetry seems to write itself. One such time was the passing of my husband of thirty-three years, and I will attempt a selection of my grief-&-loss poetry for a chapbook. My psychological practice has been enhanced by my participation in an international group studying the Sufi Tradition, as well as by frequent trips to the UK in which to study a body of practices taught by the Institute of Human Givens. Since being an adolescent, I intended to pursue creative writing; though finding my vocation within psychology, what a thrill it has been to connect again with poetry during nearly the past two decades!

walking the ocean's breath block by block
Modern Haiku 46.1

absinthe no succor in our abyss
FUG.UES 1

noon's blaze for the Angelus a cool interior
Kokako 23

swifts wheeling to the edge of dusk
Presence 53

summer magnolia buds entwined with eulogies
Otata July 2016

kimono backwards her bunraku dream
Akitsu Quarterly Winter 2017

Name **Connie Donleycott**
Volume ***A New Resonance* 4**
Residence **Bremerton WA**
Occupation **Writer**

Since appearing in *Echoes* 1 (2007), I've continued to write and enjoy haiku. One of my haiku was engraved on a boulder at The Haiku Pathway in Katikati, New Zealand. Some of my haiku have been included in the following publications *dust of summers* and *Where the Wind Turns*, both Red Moon Anthologies (edited by Jim Kacian); *Dreams Wander On* (edited by Robert Epstein); *The Temple Bell Stops* (edited by Robert Epstein); *Montage: The Book* (created and edited by Allan Burns); and, most recently, *The Wonder Code* (edited by Scott Mason).

the bunker's blackness . . .
touching its depth
with my voice
Frogpond 32.3

ebb tide —
we turn to the sound
of a whale's breath
Acorn 22

autumn's scent
in the pile of leaves . . .
I take the dare
The Heron's Nest VIII:1

spring —
paring down
to one junk drawer
The Heron's Nest XIII:1

a new year
the garbage can's lid
frozen shut
The Heron's Nest XV:2

morning light
part of a robin's egg
catches the wind
The Heron's Nest XVI:3

Name George Dorsty
Volume *A New Resonance* 3
Residence Yorktown VA
Occupation University Professor
Collections *Making Way*
The Space Between

I was chosen by vincent tripi for his pinch book series. I still love that first little book called *Making Way*. Following this I published regularly in many of the haiku publications including *The Heron's Nest, Modern Haiku, Frogpond* and *bottle rockets* and continue to do so. A few years ago Street Press on Long Island published my first chapbook of poems entitled *The Space Between*. I currently have another manuscript in preparation. I was pleased to win Favorite Senryu of issue in *Modern Haiku* three times, and to have a poem of mine included in the *Haiku in English: The First Hundred Years*. I've been honored, too, to have poems selected by poet Robert Epstein for many of his publications, and in the book of Long Island poetry, *Lights Of City And Sea*, and in several other collections as well including *The Heron's Nest's Nest Feathers*. One of my poems, "dead hamster," has been printed in several different languages and for awhile I received regular requests for it. It recently appeared again in *The Wonder Code*. I don't enter contests, so I have won no prizes except for best of issue in a few different magazines. However, I have judged a number of contests with a haiku partner. I continue to teach haiku as part of the courses I currently teach. I introduce haiku through Kerouac's *The Dharma Bums*, and Kerouac's own wonderful haiku as well as many by classic Japanese haijin, and contemporary haiku poets like the 170 *New Resonance* poets as well.

my veins turn
a deeper blue —
winter twilight

The Heron's Nest XIV:4

not in
his usual place —
the homeless man

bottle rockets 23

am I holding
them correctly?
worry beads

Modern Haiku 46.2

by the hour
my therapist's
jellybeans

Modern Haiku 47.2

low tide —
people seem
more honest

bottle rockets 25

crab bubbles
the rock sways
its seaweed

Frogpond 36.2

Name **Curtis Dunlap**
Volume ***A New Resonance* 5**
Residence **Mayodan NC**
Occupation **Systems Administrator**

I live near the confluence of the Mayo and Dan rivers in Mayodan, North Carolina. I've been published in a variety of journals including *The Christian Science Monitor, Contemporary Haibun Online, The Dead Mule School of Southern Literature, Floyd County Moonshine, Frogpond, Haibun Today, The Heron's Nest, Magnapoets, Modern Haiku, Sketchbook,* and *The Wild Goose Poetry Review*. My awards include a Museum of Haiku Literature Award in 2008; 3rd Prize in the 11th International Kusamakura Haiku Competition (2006); 1st place in the 2010 Fine Arts Festival of Rockingham County for my poem "Weekender"; and an Editors' Choice award, *The Heron's Nest* VII:4 (2005). No books published at this time but I do have a CD entitled *Another Shade of Blue*.

rocky creek bottom —
returning the worry stone
I borrowed last year

Magnapoets 1

robbing the bees
she speaks of
lip balm

The Heron's Nest XII:4

cycling with my son —
this is the autumn
I fall behind

The Heron's Nest VII:4

a rusty still
by the dry creek bed —
blood moon rising

The Heron's Nest X:1

school closings —
the snowmen arrive
flake by flake

The Heron's Nest XII:2

rain drops changing the tone of river stones

Modern Haiku 39.1

Name David Elliott
Volume *A New Resonance* 1
Residence Factoryville PA
Occupation College Professor
Collections *Wind in the Trees*
Passing Through

I was born in Minneapolis and grew up there, in New York City, and in Montclair, New Jersey. After attending Middlebury College, I received a Ph. D. in English from Syracuse University. I am currently Director of the Honors Program and Professor of English at Keystone College in La Plume, Pennsylvania. My haiku, senryu, and haibun have appeared in many journals in this country and abroad.

Alpenglow
dragonfly skimming over
the mountain's reflection
Acorn 18

between two mountains
the wings of a gliding hawk
balancing sunlight
Brussels Sprout 2.1

shielding his eyes
with his baseball glove . . .
first geese
Modern Haiku 22.2

bitter wind . . .
scraping the windshield
to find her smiling face
bottle rockets 22

so clear
here at the summit
the song of a white-throated sparrow
Frogpond 19.1

not expecting
such a moon
over my crabby neighbor's roof
Heiwa: Peace Poetry in Japanese and English

Jeanne Emrich (*A New Resonance* 2) elected not to participate in *Echoes* 2.

Name **Efren Estevez**
Volume *A New Resonance* 4
Residence **East Norwich NY**
Occupation **Food Industry Executive**

I have continued writing haiku regularly but have not been submitting work to journals or contests. My participation has been limited to the Spring Street Haiku Group which (as far as we know) is the longest continuously active haiku workshop, meeting monthly for 27 years and counting. I have edited and complied two collections of works spanning 10 years of its history, *suspiciously small* and *A Gust from the Alley*. My haiku have been informed by the wide traveling I do for my job (to places exotic and mundane), which as my fellow Spring Streeters know, keeps me away from more meetings than I would like. Previously, I was Northeast Metro Area Regional Coordinator for Haiku Society of America from 2002 – 2007, presented papers ("Troutswirl: The Nature Tradition in the Haiku of John Wills" and "An Overview of the Haiku Tradition in Spanish") at various meetings including Haiku North America (Winston-Salem, 2007). Along with having multiple articles and poems published in *Frogpond* and *Modern Haiku*, I also organized many readings of the various poets in the New York area, including the Brooklyn Botanical Gardens Annual Cherry Blossom Festival. Besides haiku, I have also published in other fields — short stories, technical computer books and other poetry forms.

Easter bells —
returning geese lost
in the bright sun
suspiciously small

going through
mom's things —
a locked drawer
suspiciously small

sauna
in the steamed window
a face from another world
suspiciously small

from the top
of a mountain trail
voices not yet words
A Gust from the Alley

in the diner window
the old man crumbles
saltines into his soup
A Gust from the Alley

the Vietnam vet
lights a joint and passes it
to a name on the wall
A Gust from the Alley

Name **Judson Evans**
Volume ***A New Resonance* 2**
Residence **Holbrook MA**
Occupation **University Professor**

Over the last 13 years, 95% of my haiku have been part of either haiga (which have become a large part of my artistic practice as objects/texts created for specific occasions and for specific individuals and then given away as "gifts" in a Buddhist spirit of non-attachment), renku (especially with my two dear friends and collaborators Raffael de Gruttola and Karen Klein), or haibun (which has been my preferred mode of writing). Since *New Resonance 2*, I have published haibun in three anthologies: *Journeys 2017: An International Haibun Anthology*, edited by Angelee Deodhar; *At the Edge: Raw NerVZ Haibun*, edited by Mike Montreuil, 2017; *Big Data: The Red Moon Anthology of English-Language Haiku*, edited by Jim Kacian & the Red Moon Editorial Staff, 2014. I continue to be an active member of The Boston Haiku Society, to teach haiku and related Japanese forms to performing artists at The Boston Conservator at Berklee, and to edit the student poetry journal *The Garden*, now in its 26th year and always a forum for students haiku, haibun, renku, and haiga. I also regularly write and publish lyric poetry and teach a course on cave painting: *The Cave: Inquiry into the Origins of Art, Philosophy, and Religion*, at The Conservatory.

September cirrus
hot tar
cooling on the roof
   Biting the Sun

spring concert
from dead wood
so much song
   The Scent of Music

bruises from a pear
most of November
gone
   Modern Haiku 42.1

a whole winter's snow
heaped on the steps —
foreclosure
   Frogpond 34.2

all the trees bare
moonlight fills
the laundry basket
   Modern Haiku 41.1

garden god
moss
in all the right places
   Wind Flow

Name **Claire Everett**
Volume *A New Resonance* 9
Residence **North Yorkshire UK**
Occupation **Writer / Editor**
Collections *twelve moons*
The Small, Wild Places
Talking in Tandem (co-author)

My haiku, tanka, haibun and tanka prose are published in journals worldwide. I was on the editorial team for *Take Five: Best Contemporary Tanka*, volume 4 (2011) and in the same year, was a contributor for cycle 11 of *DailyHaiku*. In December 2011, I became the Tanka Prose Editor at *Haibun Today*, and in 2017 UK Editor for the *Red Moon Anthology* series. 2012 saw the publication of my first collection of tanka, *twelve moons*. I have five children and two stepchildren and am happiest when walking with my husband on the North Yorkshire Moors or in the beautiful Lake District.

just-fledged light
chips of wren song
from the log pile
Presence 45

something
you're not telling me . . .
camellia buds
Acorn 28

butterfly dust . . .
the question I never
dared to ask
Acorn 27

scent of snow
unable to recall
my father's voice
The Heron's Nest XIV:3

thunderhead . . .
the buzzard's eye
fills with sky
Acorn 27

winter sun . . .
the soft flicker of waxwings
in the firethorn
The Heron's Nest XIV:1

Name: Seánan Forbes
Volume: *A New Resonance* 8
Residence: London UK
Occupation: Writer / Actor

A seventh-generation New Yorker, I moved to England in 1996. I'm a writer, photographer, storyteller, and actor. My poems have appeared in *Acorn, Sketchbook, The Mid-America Poetry Review, The Prose Poem Project, Modern Haiku, Frogpond, The Heron's Nest, Daily Haiku,* and *A Hundred Gourds*. I can usually be found in transit and am currently pursuing a PhD in creative writing, with a focus on place and poetry (haiku, senryu, tanka, haibun, and haiga).

water lilies
the weight of sunlight
on my palms
Modern Haiku 44:3

ebb tide
the night nurse
closes your eyes
Acorn 29

spring rain we leave our shadows on a stone
Modern Haiku 44.3

nesting dolls the masks behind her mask
Kernels 1

the closest thing they have
to a child
this dead cat
Modern Haiku 44:2

the cold heft of a meteorite
how far
we've come
A Neew Resonance 9

Name	Lorin Ford
Volume	*A New Resonance 7*
Residence	Melbourne Australia
Occupation	Writer
Collections	*a wattle seedpod*
	what light there is
	A Few Quick Brushstrokes

Credits include first prize for haiku in the 6th and 7th *paper wasp* Jack Stamm awards, 2005 and 2006; first prize in the Shiki Salon Annual Haiku Awards 2005, free format category; Winner and runner-ups, *The Haiku Calendar* Competition 2010; Winner, *The Haiku Calendar* Competition 2011; First prize, THF's Haiku Now! 2010 Contest (Contemporary Category); First prize, Katikati Haiku Pathway Contests, 2012 and 2014; First Prize *FreeXpresSion* Haiku Contest, 2014. Haiku readings and workshops. Haiku editor for *Notes from the Gean* (1 – 9, June 2009 – June 2011); Publisher, Haiku editor, Managing editor & other roles for *A Hundred Gourds* (December 2011 – June 2016); Founder and Convener of the Red Kelpie Haiku Group (May 2014 – present time). I live with a very stripy, very vocal, very bossy cat in a C19 workers cottage that needs repair (as I do), in what is now a trendy, inner city Melbourne suburb full of coffee shops and increasingly higher high-rise apartments. I grow my own herbs, peas, beans, greens etc. in my small front and back yards. Many birds visit and I'm on familiar terms with the local ravens. Despite rumours to the contrary, I do not use my straw broom for midnight flights over the neighbourhood.

miles
to
the
water
fall
a
river
runs
down
my
spine

Modern Haiku 45.2

slow dancing
to Satie
the pears ripen

Modern Haiku 44.1

heat shimmer
a stick on the verge
of snake

The Heron's Nest XIX:2

close to sleep the sea I slip into

paper wasp 22.2

chrysalis . . .
what will be
will be

The Heron's Nest XIV:4

dusk on the river the bunyip's cold breath

Windfall 4

Name Alice Frampton
Volume *A New Resonance* 3
Residence Seabeck WA
Occupation Person
Collections *a gate left open*
Echoes 1

I co-founded the Seabeck Haiku Getaway, volunteered as one of *The Heron's Nest* editors, and created my book, *a gate left open*, along with co-curating the first edition of *Echoes*. Oh, yeah, and hosted a few conferences along the way. I live with my mother, play with my grandchildren, make hats for the homeless, and feed my chickens. It's a hard life . . .

Earth Day
the pecking order
of chickens
The Heron's Nest XVII:3

autumn equinox
the tap tap tap
of Bingo markers
The Heron's Nest XV:1

new bathing suits
filling the boat
with laughter
The Heron's Nest XVI:3

snow . . .
the mustang in it
up to his heart
The Heron's Nest XIX:3

it is
what it is
mole hill
The Heron's Nest XV:3

Name **Chase Gagnon**
Volume *A New Resonance* 10
Residence **Harper Woods MI**
Occupation **Student**
Collection *The Sound of Shadows*

I'm a student from Michigan who grew up in a number of places in the Detroit area. I spent my high school days sitting in the back of class writing short poems and doodling on the side of my paper. Since then, my work has appeared in numerous publications and won some awards. I am also interested in mythology, folklore, and urban legends; which has somewhat inspired my poetry. My awards include Second Place in the Sharpening the Green Pencil Haiku Contest (2014); a Runner-up in the Shamrock Reader's Choice Awards (2013); and an Editor's Choice from *Cattails* (Winter 2013).

humid night . . .
a tadpole breaks the surface
of ancient stars
*Sharpening the Green Pencil 2014
Second Place*

moonless night . . .
a gypsy's finger-cymbals
pinch the stars
Under the Basho 2014

last embers
falling from the incense . . .
end of autumn
*Cattails Winter 2013
Editor's Choice*

morphine drip . . .
I sing my mother
a lullaby
Prune Juice 12

forgotten battlefield
a crash of thunder
shakes the grass
Shamrock 24

her ashes
settle in the pond
starry night
Learning to See the Truth

Name: Jack Galmitz
Volume: *A New Resonance* 4
Residence: New York NY
Occupation: Retired
Collections: *For a Sparrow*
The Coincidence of Stars
Balanced Is the Rose

It's been quite some time since I have published or sought to publish haiku in any of the available forums. I have been publishing some free verse and haiku occasionally in *otata*, an online blog belonging to John Martone. I think what remains of haiku as an active part of my life is my love of sparrows. I wrote a book published in Macedonia titled *For A Sparrow* that was dedicated to my father, now deceased. The inscription of the book was *Father/ on the road to god none fail/ let's start here*. And if you aren't aware of it, in Paris sparrows will feed from your hand: you can feel the warmth of their bodies as they linger to eat just ever so shortly.

Ussachevsky where are you
I have a tape recorder
Coordinates

Water skiing
well, I'm no Jesus
Coordinates

The handball court
a language of sorts
Coordinates

The infield is diamond shaped
as it should be
Coordinates

Tribal drums
my heart thumps
Coordinates

Sundown over snow
look at that blue
Coordinates

Name **Brenda J. Gannam**
Volume ***A New Resonance* 4**
Residence **Brooklyn NY**
Occupation **Writer / Consultant**

No update.

> among
> mother's old love letters
> not one from dad
> *Five O'Clock Shadow*

after the divorce
the first time
I hear my maiden name
The Pianist's Nose

> midnight subway
> watching her apply lipstick
> he licks his lips
> *lit from within*

sculpture gallery
the kids try to peek
behind the fig leaves
behind the fig leaves

> peeling boiled eggs
> she daydreams
> of a long lost lover
> *Erotic Haiku*

after the funeral
slipping my bare feet
into Dad's old shoes
unpublished

Name: Barry George
Volume: *A New Resonance 2*
Residence: Philadelphia PA
Occupation: College Professor
Collections: *Wrecking Ball*
The One That Flies Back

I've published *Wrecking Ball and Other Urban Haiku* (Accents Publishing) and *The One That Flies Back* (Kattywompus Press), a chapbook of tanka. My poems have appeared in leading haiku journals, including translations into twelve languages, as well as in the anthologies/collections *A New Resonance 2: Emerging Voices in English-Language Haiku*; *The New Haiku*; *Haiku 21*; *Kamesan's World Haiku Anthology on War, Violence and Human Rights Violations*; *Something out of Nothing*; and *Bigger Than They Appear: Anthology of Very Short Poems*. An AWP Intro Poets Award recipient and Pushcart nominee, I've won numerous Japanese short-form competitions, including First Prize in the Gerald R. Brady Senryu Contest. I've also presented haiku workshops to learners of all ages, from second grade through college and beyond.

for I who go
for you who stay —
two inaugurations
  Modern Haiku 48.1

how long
does a human footprint last . . .
the summer moon
  Haiku Canada Anthology 2015

unweeded, overgrown
I sit among them —
autumn marigolds
  Kō 28.4

memorials
on the courthouse plaza —
room for maybe one more war
  Ershik 8

once before you go
receding snow bank —
tell me your secrets
  Betty Drevniok Award
  3rd Place

the vagrant
reasoning with someone
who isn't there
  Haiku Canada Review 5.1

Name	Beverley George
Volume	*A New Resonance* 4
Residence	Pearl Beach Australia
Occupation	Retired
Collections	*Spinifex*
	The Birds That Stay

I began writing haiku in 1997. My haiku pathway has taken me to Japan to follow in the footsteps of Bashō on six small group travel journeys as literary adviser to Mitsui Travel. I presented papers at two conferences in Japan, and a workshop in New Zealand and have served as an international judge for several competitions. One of my main roles has been to edit haiku journals: *Yellow Moon; Young Yellow Moon* and *Windfall: Australian Haiku*. I also founded a tanka journal *Eucalypt* and edited the first 21 issues over a period of ten years. I was President of the Australian Haiku Society (2006–10) and in September 2009 convened the 4-day Fourth Haiku Pacific Rim Conference in Terrigal, NSW, attended by international delegates from UK, US, Canada, Japan and New Zealand as well as many fellow Australian haiku enthusiasts. Over years, haiku and tanka have played an integral part of my daily life. I particularly enjoy the way in which the genre can be shared, as in haiga, renga, ginko and small groups that meet regularly. I enjoy surprises and was pleased to learn one of my haiku was selected by the British Haiku Society for printing on a scarf for the Silks and Haiku exhibition at the St Pancras Crypt Gallery September 2011. Another was when Janice Bostok and I were invited to submit 15 haiku each for inclusion in an enjoyable electronic game titled Haiku Journey, now published by Big Fish Games. My first book of haiku, *Spinifex*, was published by Pardalote Press in 2006 and my haiku chapbook *The Birds That Stay* (Eucalypt, 2013) was re-published on The Haiku Foundation web-site.

from a lifted oar
a shimmer connects the sky
and sunlit river
<small>Genkissu Haiku Contest 2009
1st Prize</small>

closing day
vine tomatoes
warm my hands
<small>Kaji Aso Contest 2011
2nd Prize</small>

parsley bed
the stretched necks
of snails
<small>Katikati Contest 2014
Highly Commended</small>

tsunami dreams —
grass pillows for the homeless
on Bashō's *Narrow Road*
<small>Kusamakura Contest 2011
2nd Prize</small>

opera in the park
a kookaburra takes on
the tenor
<small>*Blithe Spirit* 27.2</small>

fireside knitting
the unfinished scarf
around my neck
<small>*The Birds That Stay*</small>

Name **Lee Giesecke**
Volume *A New Resonance* 1
Residence **Annandale VA**
Occupation **Retired**

I am still writing — maybe a bit less — and have been sending stuff to *bottle rockets, Modern Haiku, Frogpond,* and *The Heron's Nest*. I have also been lucky enough to appear in the *Red Moon Anthology* a few times (2009, 2012, 2016), as well as three other post-publication anthologies: *lanterns: a firefly anthology* (bottle rockets press, 2007), *seed packets: an anthology of flower haiku* (bottle rockets press, 2010), and *Every Chicken, Cow, Fish and Frog: Animal Rights Haiku* (2016). I have also had fun incorporating haiku brevity, line breaks, and stanza lengths into some of my longer poetry.

power outage
the neighbor's fireflies
still on
Frogpond 39.2

bomb in the Metro
petals in a
clear glass bowl
Modern Haiku 47.1

Ah, Christmas . . .
a choir of a hundred
singing rumpa pum pum
Towpath Anthology 2010

summer day . . .
the cloud that didn't move
gone
The Heron's Nest XIV:4

snow everywhere
and its stillness
inside of me
Brussels Sprout VIII:3

Beethoven
seeing the bell
not ring
bottle rockets 22

Name **Robert Gilliland**
Volume ***A New Resonance* 1**
Residence **Austin TX**
Occupation **Retired**
Collections ***mosquitoes and moonlight***
from somewhere upstream

My first collection, *mosquitoes and moonlight*, was selected as one of the winners of the Virgil Hutton Memorial Haiku Chapbook Contest. My second collection, *from somewhere upstream*, won the Snapshot Press Book Award 2016. In 2016 I was invited to read at the Two Autumns Poetry Reading sponsored by the Haiku Poets of Northern California. Some of my poems have won the Museum of Haiku Literature Award, *Modern Haiku* Editor's Choice Award, *The Heron's Nest* Editors' Choice Award, and the Snapshot Press Calendar Competition. Poems have been included in the following anthologies: *A New Resonance 1, The Red Moon Anthology, Nest Feathers, An Amazement of Deer,* and *Haiku in English: The First Hundred Years* as well as *Haiku: A Poet's Guide* and *The Wonder Code*. From 2004 to 2008 I served as an Associate Editor of *The Heron's Nest*. I am profoundly grateful for having stumbled upon haiku. Its way of experiencing the world and its Sangha of wonderfully diverse poets enrich, inspire and enlighten me on a continual basis.

the soft splash
of a lap swimmer's strokes
morning coolness
Acorn 39

small scars
where the vine once held them
autumn tomatoes
Modern Haiku 48.2

mirrored mountain . . .
in and out of the stillness
a trout's silver skin
Acorn 35

evening glow —
the last holdout surrenders
their treehouse fort
The Heron's Nest XVII:3

stubble field —
a hawk and its shadow
meet at the mouse
Modern Haiku 46.1

whispers
about a neighbor's wife run off
— first firefly
Modern Haiku 45.3

Name **Kate S. Godsey**
Volume ***A New Resonance* 9**
Residence **Pacifica CA**
Occupation **Psychotherapist**

No update.

> waiting
> for the other shoe
> blue rain
> *bottle rockets* 26

islands of light
on a vast gray sea
how much time is left
Whirligig 2.2

> stealth of raccoons
> the intimacy of
> a shared solitude
> *World Haiku Review* 2012

apple blossoms
the easy forgiveness
of children
A Hundred Gourds 2.2

> low tide
> space where the ache
> used to be
> *Frogpond* 35.3

all day
sensing plums ripen
it's you, again
unpubllished

Name **Chris Gordon**
Volume ***A New Resonance* 1**
Residence **Eugene OR**
Occupation **Teacher**
Collections ***Cucumbers Are Related to Lemons***
An Apparent Definition of Wavering

I started the journal *ant ant ant ant ant* in 1994. My haiku have appeared in numerous journals and anthologies over the past 25 years, including *A Guide to Haiku for the 21st Century*, *Haiku 21: An Anthology of Contemporary English-language Haiku*, and *Haiku in English: The First Hundred Years*. My enduring favorites include Matsuo Allard, Gary Hotham, M. Kettner, Marlene Mountain, and Hiroaki Sato. I teach history and literature to middle and high school students at a mental health treatment school. I have a particular fondness for science fiction written in the 1960s and 70s. I studied Greek and Latin in college. I met Robert Bly once. He was very kind.

it's a kind of light leaf shadows
is/let 2016

the cats the way they are with cats
is/let 2014

casting a shadow on
the ceiling a crane fly
stuck to the bulb
Bones 4

across the valley
controlled burns
converge
is/let 2016

I didn't miscalculate I was just incorrect
is/let 2016

and then we can read about Mars she says
is/let 2014

Name **David Grayson**
Volume *A New Resonance* 6
Residence **Alameda CA**
Occupation **Product Manager**
Collection *Discovering Fire*

I've been writing haiku since 1998. My first book, *Discovering Fire: Haiku & Essays*, was published by Red Moon Press in 2016. I served as Editor of *Full of Moonlight*, the Haiku Society of America 2016 Members' Anthology. I was Editor of two editions of the Two Autumns book series: *Moonlight Changing Direction* in 2008 and *The Half-Finished Bridge* in 2014. I was a featured poet in the 2009 Two Autumns book, *My Neighbor*. I live in the San Francisco Bay Area with my family. In addition to haiku, I write about poetry and literature in general. Besides writing, I enjoy the outdoors and am active in the Boy Scouts.

the muezzin's voice
breaks on the high note
Ramadan moon
Frogpond 40.3

I blink and the fox disappears —
scent of wildflower
Modern Haiku 45.3

first day of school
his backpack
filled with summer
Shiki Kukai September 2009

the old man pushes
his wheelchair down the street
sound of the wind
Mariposa 36

memorial candle
the smoke
turning into air
Mariposa 24

layoffs —
the indents from the chair
still in the carpet
Frogpond 33.2

Name **Andrea Grillo**
Volume *A New Resonance* 6
Residence **Randolph NJ**
Occupation **Visual Artist**

My haiku life is now a quiet one — mostly for my own personal enjoyment. I publish my haiku along with haibun and other forms of poetry and prose on my blog "The Poetry of Soil". I delight in the paint and poetry of messy and storms, haiku and *wabi sabi*. I am working toward the practice of a creative alchemy that rises and transforms an imperfect line into a stroke that finds its way to poetic expression. And I am truly grateful for the community of poets and artists who continue to support and inspire our creative voices. Please have a look at my art website.

desert thunder —
in the hands of the artist
turquoise and silver

Frogpond 40.2

Name **Kay Grimnes**
Volume ***A New Resonance* 3**
Residence **Alma MI**
Occupation **Retired Biology Professor**

No update.

                    thunderhead
                    a mass of starlings
                    splits in two
                          Frogpond 26.2

    becalmed
    a cottonwood puff sails
    into the boat
        GEPPO XXIV:4

                    sprinklers on the sidewalk
                    the girl in the wheelchair
                    times her run
                          RAW NerVZ III:2

    retirement party
    maple seeds spin slowly
    to the driveway
        The Heron's Nest IV:10

                    cloudless night
                    a drip in the sink
                    catches the moon
                          Acorn 5

    first snow
    the baby's fingers
    close around nothing
        South by Southeast IX:3

Name Carolyn Hall
Volume *A New Resonance 2*
Residence San Francisco CA
Occupation Writer
Collections *Water Lines*
How to Paint the Finch's Song
The Doors All Unlocked
Calculus of Daylilies

I discovered haiku in 1999, and haiku and the haiku community have been important elements of my life ever since. I have served as an officer of the Haiku Poets of Northern California (HPNC) for many years. For four years I was the editor of *Acorn*. Currently I am editor of *Mariposa*, the membership journal of HPNC. Over the past twenty years my haiku have received awards from the Haiku Society of America, the Snapshot Press Haiku Calendar Competition, the Robert Spiess competition, the Peggy Willis Lyles haiku contest, and *The Heron's Nest* Readers' Choice Poem of the Year, among others. My poems have also appeared in numerous anthologies, including *Haiku in English: The First Hundred Years* (W.W. Norton, 2013). My most recent book, *Calculus of Daylilies*, was published in 2017 by Red Moon Press. My three previous full-length collections of haiku are: *Water Lines* (Snapshot Press 2006, co-winner of the Snapshot Press Book Award), *How to Paint the Finch's Song* (Red Moon Press 2010, First Place in The Haiku Foundation Touchstone Distinguished Book Awards), and *The Doors All Unlocked* (Red Moon Press 2012, First Place in the HSA Merit Books Awards and HM in the Touchstone Distinguished Book Awards). A city mouse / country mouse, I divide my time between San Francisco and the rural outskirts of Santa Rosa, California.

her eighth decade
how the rains
rearrange the creek
Mariposa 34

prize pumpkin
it doesn't matter
what I weigh
The Haiku Calendar 2015

death what kind of plan is that
Mariposa 35

a password
to access my passwords
the hummingbird's tongue
Lyles Haiku Contest 2014
First Place

on demand summer sky reruns
Modern Haiku 46.3

Voyager 1
enters interstellar space
the cat's closed eyes
Frogpond 37.1

Name Jeffrey Harpeng
Volume *A New Resonance* 3
Residence Moorooka Australia
Occupation Mac Operator
Collection *Quarter Past Sometime*

No update.

        sleet drifting
        in the burnt-out house
        a bird cage
           Takahe 36

piercing cold —
I forcew
the rusty hinge
  The New Zealand Haiku Anthology

        yellowed sheet music
        mother's voice
        and some words
          The Second New Zealand Haiku Anthology

her shadow
draws a blanket
across the window
  Still 1

        stained glass light
        fills
        the collection plate
          paper wasp summer 2002

in her sign language
autumn
becomes fall
  unpublished

Name **Michele L. Harvey**
Volume *A New Resonance* 8
Residence **Hamilton NY**
Occupation **Professional Painter**

I began to write haiku just after the Autumn of 2005, when I got my first computer. I'd been aware of haiku since grade school but was unaware there was a contemporary haiku world. Since then I have gone on to be awarded both national and international awards. There are too many to list here, but the first was the Herold G. Henderson Award in 2010 (judges: Fay Aoyagi & Lenard D. Moore) and the last was Golden Haiku Award 2017, in which I was named the Global Award Winner (judge: John Stevenson.) Being a landscape painter by trade, my life has been divided equally between a quiet rural life in Hamilton, NY and an urban life in Brooklyn, NY. Both these environments inform and shape my painting and my haiku. Nature is often equated with a country setting but may be found in the heart of city life too, if one pays close attention. The natural world feels far away and nearly unreachable there, but haiku (like my painting,) serves as anchor to my very core, of nature.

Mother's Day—
lilacs fill
the void

The Heron's Nest XVII:3

rutting season . . .
surveyor's stakes
mark what's ours

The Heron's Nest XVIII:4

teasing the tightness
out of the buds
spring sun

The Heron's Nest XIX:2

their ancient hum
to sunrise
honeybees

The Heron's Nest XIX:3

spring fever
the farm gate swung wide
for the bull

The Heron's Nest XIX:4

heaping manure
around the roses . . .
spring equinox

Golden Haiku Contest 2017
Winner, Global Award

Name **John Hawk**
Volume *A New Resonance* 8
Residence **Hilliard OH**
Occupation **Communications Professional**

Haiku continues to be a part of my life, however sporadically and unpredictably, typically brought on by some change in circumstances or by random coincidence. After a near five-year hiatus, it's been refreshing to let the "haiku moment" happen rather than forcing something that's not there. I've had some success with competitions and submissions since returning to the genre and hope to someday publish a full collection of my work, but now I'm mostly enjoying the simple satisfaction of new experiences and the careful preservation of these moments through haiku.

fishing
he brings up
Jesus
UHTS Contest 2017
Second Place

the moon
almost empty
winter rain
The Heron's Nest XIX:2

scattered stars shaking off the umbrella
Acorn 39

humming to myself the river
Modern Haiku 48.3

frantic ants
still building
the unlit fire
tinywords 17.1

Oh snail,
how was Mt. Fuji
on the way down?
Failed Haiku 17

Name **Jeff Hoagland**
Volume *A New Resonance* 7
Residence **Hopewell NJ**
Occupation **Naturalist**

I practice haiku as an antidote to a busy life and to stay connected to the "real" world. My haiku have appeared in a wide range of journals and anthologies, and awards include: Third Place Haiku Foundation Facebook Contest 2010; Honorable Mention ITO EN Oi-ocha New Haiku Contest 2011; Honorable Mention Kaji Aso Studio Haiku Contest 2013; Third Prize Anita Weiss Haiku Award 2013; and Honorable Mention Kaji Aso Studio Haiku Contest 2014. Since 2013, I've facilitated ginkos as part of International Haiku Poetry Day at the Watershed Reserve in NJ and for the Haiku Society of America Northeast Metro Group in New York City. I consider my work "mission work", utilizing the LEED-Platinum Watershed Center and the surrounding 950-acre nature reserve as an effective platform for teaching about the environment. As a naturalist, I enjoy a very public love affair with all things wild and am perhaps most at home in a stream or river; exploring the darkness of night; communing with little creatures; or sharing time in nature with my family. I began my haiku journey ten years ago, noting the shared viewpoint of the naturalist and the haiku poet.

hide-and-seek
the forest trail
in autumn
bottle rockets 28

autumn chill
the acorn
missing its cap
Frogpond 35.1

peach season
the cloud
in my kitchen
Mayfly 62

one page
ahead of me
housefly
Acorn 36

mourning cloak
pausing to catch
its shadow
Akitsu Quarterly Spring 2017

mulberry stains
my fingers
on your lips
Modern Haiku 48.2

Name   Paul Hodder
Volume   *A New Resonance* 6
Residence   Melbourne Australia
Occupation   Airline Onboard Manager

Haiku has been part of my life since I started meditating. I wanted to somehow distill the "suchness" of the moment into written form. I have taught haiku to my daughter's English class on a few occasions. I have also read at a couple of poetry nights in cafes in Melbourne. I have been published on various websites including *Haibun Today* and also "Now this: contemporary poems of beginnings, renewals and firsts." I was a regular participant in the Shiki monthly Kukai which forced me to work my haiku muscles on a regular basis. I was born in England and have now lived more than half of my life in Australia. I have been very fortunate to work in a job I love for almost 30 years, flying to international destinations on a weekly basis. The time I get to spend in places such as Japan and Hong Kong gives me lots of opportunity to practice meditation and write haiku whilst getting inspiration from the different cultures. However, my favourite destination is home where my greatest muses are — my wife Carla and daughter Mia.

back to school
the smoothness of a shell
in her pocket
<small>Shiki Kukai 13 June
Second Place</small>

first taste
of ice cream
— her eyes
<small>Shiki Kukai 12 May
First Place</small>

as if
he's lost something
egret in the reeds
<small>Shiki Kukai 15 November
Third Place</small>

buddha's birthday
more shoes than spaces
on the temple steps
<small>Shiki Kukai 13 June
First Place</small>

reflected
in the traffic cop's sunglasses
her best smile
<small>Shiki Kukai 15 January
Second Place</small>

all their
little beating hearts
migration
<small>Shiki Kukai 16 April
Third Place</small>

Name **Mark Hollingsworth**
Volume ***A New Resonance* 4**
Residence **Gustine CA**
Occupation **Pastor**

No update.

        new year's day
        listening to the tub fill
        from under water
            unpublished

in the snowy path
one set of footprints
I stretch my stride
   Mariposa 11

        hospital hallway
        this far
        and no further
            Frogpond 27.3

lightning . . .
the flash of your photograph
at my bedside
   Feel of the Handrail

        some mist
        off of the waterfall
        falls on her toes
            HSA Members' Anthology 2004

autumn dusk
at the end of the lane
only a chimney
   Hermitage 1

Name **Cara Holman**
Volume ***A New Resonance* 9**
Residence **Portland OR**
Occupation **Retired**

I am happy to call the Pacific Northwest my home for the past 26 years now. My haiku have been featured in *Frogpond, The Heron's Nest, Notes From the Gean, A Hundred Gourds, Modern Haiku, tinywords, Mariposa, Acorn, Prune Juice, DailyHaiku, Sketchbook, RMA 2012, RMA 2013*, and most recently, *The Wonder Code*. My awards include placings in the Vancouver Cherry Blossom Festival Haiku Invitational, the International Kusamakura Haiku Competition, the Porad Award, the HIA Haiku Contest, the *Mainichi* Haiku Contest, and the HaikuNow! International Haiku Contest. These days I am reading through my large collection of haiku books, and still keeping a hand in writing haiku as well.

fine mist
he says frogs
I say crickets
The Heron's Nest XIII:3

daydreaming
thistledown drifts
on the breeze
Notes from the Gean 3.1

barefoot summer . . .
a drop of honeysuckle
on my tongue
Standing Still

flickering stars
my old bedroom
now a study
Notes from the Gean 3.1

muted sunlight
the crisp corners
of the folded flag
The Heron's Nest XII:2

starting over —
my footprints erased
by the morning tide
Frogpond 34.1

Name Elizabeth Howard
Volume *A New Resonance* 1
Residence Bartlett TN
Occupation Retired

My first haiku was published in 1990, one haiku in the *Haiku Quarterly*. I have been writing haiku ever since. For the last few years, however, I have written more tanka than haiku. I do not enter contests, etc. I live in Tennessee where very few people write haiku.

filling the birdbath —
a rust-colored toad washes
out of the overflow
Cattails May 2016

interlocking lakes
a bald eagle rises
with its prey
Modern Haiku 47.2

spring fever . . .
a grizzled mare rolls
in the sprouting grass
Frogpond 38.1

night fog —
an occasional twitter
in the screech owl's oak
A Hundred Gourds 4.3

through a hole
in the storm-tossed forest
the broken moon
A Hundred Gourds 4.4

on a clear day fuzz on the mantel
Modern Haiku 46.2

Name **Jon Iddon**
Volume ***A New Resonance* 3**
Residence **Harrogate England**
Occupation **Physician**

No update.

                                    end of the breeze —
                                    a flag returns
                                    to its shadow
                                        unpublished

        end of the sale
        a pile
        of naked dummies
            unpublished

                                    low sun across the sea —
                                    the light
                                    in the jellyfish
                                        unpublished

        land breeze —
        a child's scarf flutters
        out to sea
            Presence 19

                                    offloading luggage
                                    on the station platform
                                    shadows building
                                        Blithe Spirit 12.2

        through my stethoscope
        the rumble
        of the 8:15
            Frogpond 26.2

Name **Keiko Izawa**
Volume ***A New Resonance* 5**
Residence **Yokohama Japan**
Occupation **Retired**

No update.

                        flipping the remaining pages
                            of the calendar
                                september wind
                                  Clouds Peak 2

high school reunion
we view the falling leaves
in different ways
    The Heron's Nest IX:3

                        morning dew . . .
                        in the autumn wind
                        a newborn's cry
                              Haiku Harvest Fall 2005

ice skating
into his hand
my whole weight
    Simply Haiku winter 2005

                        cold night
                        I quietly loosen
                        the guitar's strings
                              Presence 30

pounding rain —
  realizing I'm on
    the wrong train
    unpublished

Name **Duro Jaiye**
Volume *A New Resonance* 7
Residence Hirakata Japan
Occupation EFL Lecturer

My haiku activities have included:
- Serving as editor of *Icebox* (The Hailstone Haiku Circle Blog; Kyoto, Japan) from 2012 – present;
- conducting haiga walks, workshops, and lectures, for Hailstone Haiku Circle (Kyoto, Japan) from 2006 – present;
- earning Honorable Mention in the Reichhold Haiga Competiton 2016;
- being included in *galaxy of dust: The Red Moon Anthology of English-Language Haiku* 2015;
- receiving Second Prize in the Turtle Light Press Chapbook Competition 2012;
- taking Second Prize in The Robert Spiess Memorial 2012 Haiku Award.

pure silence
on the other side of the window
night snow
Akitsu Quarterly Winter 2017

from heaven
a hummingbird arrives
to taste our garden
Presence 59

blue notes:
a long day
of soft rain
Acorn 39

war talk . . .
a sudden wind
scatters the leaves
Chrysanthemum 19

on a mountain
facing the sea
family tombs
Modern Haiku 47.2

nightwalk
on this remote island
the animal in us
Frogpond 39.1

Name **Jennifer Jensen**
Volume *A New Resonance* **1**
Residence **Fair Oaks CA**
Occupation **Technical Writer**

No update.

spring rain
above the dam
almost silence
evening thunder

Monday morning
brushing sand
from between the sheets
Frogpond 21.2

the sun's warmth
storefront mannequins
also changing clothes
unpublished

summer's end
wild raspberries
dried on the stem
unpublished

resting her head
on the shoulder strap
the long ride home
unpublished

early darkness
bookmarking "winter"
in my *saijiki*
unpublished

Name **Jörgen Johansson**
Volume *A New Resonance* 6
Residence Lidköping Sweden
Occupation Retired
Collections *the firefly's signature*
half way through
wishbone
Mud on the Wall

No update.

dusk...
spitting out the rotten part
of the apple
Acorn 18

the transvestite
hesitates for a second
at the airport restrooms
Simply Haiku 3.3

dazzled by
the long distance skates
on her shoulder
Modern Haiku 38.1

scattered showers
a preschool class disappears
into the forest
Mainichi Daily News 2005

heatwave —
nuns take turns
at the drinking fountain
The Heron's Nest VII:3

a ladybird
b5 to c4
Haiku in English

Name **P M F Johnson**
Volume *A New Resonance* **9**
Residence **Minneapolis MN**
Occupation **Writer**

I have placed over 100 haiku, mostly in traditional magazines — *Modern Haiku, Frogpond, Mayfly, The Heron's Nest*, and so on. Many have been reprinted, in such anthologies as *Haiku 21, The Temple Bell*, and the *Red Moon Anthologies*. I am married to the beautiful and brilliant writer, Sandra Rector. We go for walks of discovery nearly every day.

sanctuary city —
Canada geese
on our grass
Modern Haiku 48.3

bridge over
the tidal flats —
starting chemo
Modern Haiku 48.2

playground half
the size I remember —
scattered leaves
The Heron's Nest XIX:2

picnic
lightning
how many seconds
The Heron's Nest XVIII:3

after the stroke —
the tea in his cup
trembling
Frogpond 38.3

beginning
the kiss
at the nape
Frogpond 38.2

Name **Colin Stewart Jones**
Volume *A New Resonance 7*
Residence *Aberdeen Scotland*
Occupation *Writer / Editor*
Collections *Catch 41*
Black Label
Four Virtual Haiku Poets

No update.

      hazy moon . . .
      I remind myself
      that memory lies
         unpublished

north wind
I feel first snow
in your grip
   paper wasp 12.2

      we both squeeze
      through the kissing gate . . .
      thunderclap
         The Heron's Nest XI:4

Dachau —
the old man's
adam's apple
   A Seal Snorts Out the Moon

      hangover . . .
      out-of-date condiments
      rattle in my fridge
         Frogpond 32.2

no moon
my mind follows
   the wild geese
   Simply Haiku 7.2

Name **Elmedin Kadric**
Volume *A New Resonance* **10**
Residence **Helsingborg Sweden**
Occupation **Administrator**
Collection ***buying time***

No update.

a little something left in the grass parts returning home
is/let April 8 2017

marble hallway   our rubber soles
Frogpond 40.3

in puddles
stars coming up
for air
Acorn 39

as
an

ex
am
ple

in
aut
umn
Otata 22

wild
the sun
on horseback
The Heron's Nest XIX:3

from monologue
to dialogue
the river enters the sea
Hedgerow 119

Name **Kirsty Karkow**
Volume *A New Resonance* 3
Residence Waldoboro ME
Occupation Retired
Collections *A Net of Sunlight*
water poems
shorelines

I live somewhere on the rocky coast of Maine in a Danish cottage between the ocean and a large pond. Most of my life has been prescribed by the watery aspects of nature, which often influence my poetry. Having journeyed through many passions and interests I now find that my happiest days are those spent at home, quietly mucking about outside and indoors... and laughing with my husband, Ed. My awards include numerous Second Prize, Third Prize, and Honorable Mention awards in a variety of contests such as the Yellow Moon Seed Pearls Contest, the Mainichi Haiku Contest, the RH Blyth Award, and The Robert Spiess Memorial Haiku Award Competition.

gnarled oak
my path to the hills
starts in mist
Modern Haiku 32.3

still arguing
we swim the same river
further upstream
shorelines

evening mist —
square-rigged ships
fade out of sight
Kusamakura Haiku Contest 2004
Third Place

returning geese
dawn rises over the rim
of my coffee cup
R H Blyth Award 2002
Winner

blue sky
I almost miss
the morning glory
Frogpond 24.2

guttering candle...
a whole life lived without
the Northern Lights
The Heron's Nest XI:4

Name **Bill Kenney**
Volume *A New Resonance* 5
Residence **Whitestone NY**
Occupation **Retired English Prof**
Collections *the earth pushes back*
senior admission

I wrote my first haiku in December 2004, one month short of my seventy-second birthday. Several months passed before I began to send haiku and senryu out for possible publication, but since that time, I have published my work in many leading haiku journals. If my count is correct, my work has been included in twelve of the last thirteen iterations of the *Red Moon Anthology of English-Language Haiku*. My first book, *the earth pushes back*, was published by Red Moon Press in 2016. It was granted honorable mention in the Touchstone Awards of that year. A second book, *Senior Admission*, also published by Red Moon Press, is to be published in spring 2018. In August 2018 I'll be reading at the Two Autumns Haiku Reading series in San Francisco. I retired from full time teaching at Manhattan College in 1998. My wife Pat and I live in the borough of Queens in New York City. She is a native New Yorker; I was raised in the Boston area. I have two sons from an earlier marriage and two grandchildren, who occasionally turn up in my poems. I'm an active member of the Spring Street haiku group in New York City and Inkstone Poetry online. My most recent birthday places me firmly among the "old old," and I value ever more strongly the companionship of the haiku community, including those I haven't met yet.

undocumented
he shows me pictures
of his children
Failed Haiku March 2017

starving children
. . .
switching channels
Frogpond 39.3

the doctor wants
to take a closer look
my unexamined life
Notes from the Gean 1.1

her suicide . . .
the church full of people
I think I know
Modern Haiku 46.2

Indian summer
was I ever the man
I used to be
The Heron's Nest XIX:3

barefoot
the earth
pushes back
Acorn 21

Name: Michael Ketchek
Volume: *A New Resonance* 1
Residence: Rochester NY
Occupation: Retired Day Care Teacher
Collections: *Over Our Heads*
Bases Loaded
Laughing to Myself
last gingko leaf

Since 1986 when one of my haiku was published in *Modern Haiku* lots of my haiku have appeared in various journals and anthologies. A few years ago I started a small publishing company Free Food Press and have published books by various poets including Tom Clausen whose book won the HSA Merit book award. My latest publication is a novel/haibun I wrote called *Haiku Detective* which is a mystery featuring a haiku writing detective. I am just an old hippie, hiking in the woods, listening to all sorts of music, writing my poems and hoping for a better world than the one we live in now.

deep woods
the half hour of sun
the little pine gets
Acorn 38

second chorus of boos
the shortstop drops the ball
on the scoreboard replay
bottle rockets 35

turning sixty
all I can do
is waterproof my boots
bottle rockets 37

fuck you
oh. excuse me
I was talking to God
bottle rockets 32

cold morning rain —
there is just no way to blame
the dead rat
Modern Haiku 47.2

fresh snow
the small tracks left
by a skittering leaf
Frogpond 38.2

Name **Deborah P Kolodji**
Volume *A New Resonance 4*
Residence **Temple City CA**
Occupation **Senior Technical Consultant**
Collection *highway of sleeping towns*

In 2016 my first full length book of haiku, *highway of sleeping towns*, was published by Shabda Press, which went on to win a Touchstone Distinguished Book Award and an Honorable Mention in the Haiku Society of America's Kanterman Book Awards. I read from the book at Poets House (NYC) and it was included in the 2017 Poets House Showcase. In 2013, I co-organized (with Naia) Haiku North America on the *Queen Mary* in Long Beach, California, and was named to the Board of Directors for Haiku North America in 2016. In 2013, one of my speculative haiku won the Dwarf Stars Award from the Science Fiction and Fantasy Poetry Association and was published in the *2015 Nebula Award Showcase* by the Science Fiction and Fantasy Writers of America. I currently serve as the HSA California Regional Coordinator. Now that the kids are grown and living on their own, I indulge in a few "haiku trips" a year. Two of my three offspring are also published haiku poets. I enjoy botanical gardens, visiting National Parks and independent bookstores, walking on the beach, and bird walks at the Bolsa Chica Ecological Preserve.

what's left of us
caves
on Mars
Modern Haiku 46.3

Mount Vesuvius
    the broken gear
on the time machine
Haiku Canada Review 10.1

this and that dandelion thoughts
Modern Haiku 48.2

ignoring the eviction notice mud dauber
Acorn 39

a bullfrog
hits the lower register
weeping willow song
tinywords 1 October 2015

prickly pear
blossoms still unopened
the celibate years
Mariposa 37

Name **Robert Kusch**
Volume ***A New Resonance* 2**
Residence **Camden NJ**
Occupation **Retired**
Collection ***The Field***

> not knowing their names
> not wanting to
> . . . a day of tall trees
> *Tundra* 1

bullet train —
all the stillness left behind
chasing it
Frogpond 22.2

> tall as his shack
> the hermit's woodpile
> — late October wind
> *Gathering Light*

hammering
the tent peg . . .
how close the stars
South by Southeast 5.3

> after the funeral —
> in grandfather's toolshed
> his sharpened scythe
> *Northwest Literary Forum* 17

fresh apple-core
on the compost pile;
soft October rain
Modern Haiku 25.1

Name **Marcus Larsson**
Volume ***A New Resonance* 5**
Residence **Växjö Sweden**
Occupation **Design Manager**
Collection ***Dad's Accordion***

No update.

        spring morning
        the children's game
        of being quiet
            The Heron's Nest VI:12

April argument
we can't suppress
our laughter
   Frogpond 27.1

        spring sunshine
        the ladder i brought you
        left behind
            Modern Haiku 36.2

smell of matches
we recall the movies
that made us scared
   The Heron's Nest VII:12

        snowy evening
        no lights in the house
        where there are problems
            Frogpond 30.1

spring planting
caught smiling at me
you won't say why
   Modern Haiku 38.2

Name **Catherine JS Lee**
Volume *A New Resonance* 7
Residence **Eastport ME**
Occupation **HS Special Educator**
Collection *All That Remains*

I have not written or submitted haiku for a long time. I did publish a haibun, "Wild Strawberries," in *Contemporary Haibun Online* in April, 2016. My haiga have appeared at *Daily Haiga*, and in Kuniharu Shimizu's World Haiku Association Haiga Contest. Since my appearance in *A New Resonance* 7, I have taught haiku workshops at The Haiku Circle in Northfield, Massachusetts (2013), and Calais Bookshop in Calais, Maine (2014); edited and designed the Haiku Society of America's 2015 members' anthology, *A Splash of Water*; did haiku readings with Bruce Ross and the Bangor Haiku Group at Coastal Botanical Gardens in Boothbay, Maine, and libraries in Portland, Camden, and Bangor, Maine; and presented a haiga slide show and haiku reading from my prize-winning chapbook, *All That Remains*, at the University of Maine at Machias as part of their Maine Writers Series (2014), and at the first annual Milbridge Lit Fest in Milbridge, Maine (2017). I started writing haiku during my husband's final illness, and it became my solace. Since his passing, I haven't written much at all. Although I do participate in events when I'm invited, even thinking about haiku still makes me sad. I am working to resolve these feelings so I can start writing again, because I truly do miss being part of the haiku world and I feel I still have something to say.

his scythe
murmurs in the grass . . .
grandfather's stories
All That Remains

pasture cairn
the old farmer's
bent spine
All That Remains

summer night
a freighter's horn lengthens
through the night
All That Remains

again he sighs
and tells her his name
afternoon fog
All That Remains

horseshoes and gossip
tossed around the grove
family reunion
All That Remains

deepening dusk
a great blue heron
fades to sky
All That Remains

Name **Marcus Liljedahl**
Volume ***A New Resonance* 10**
Residence **Gothenburg Sweden**
Occupation **Opera Singer**
Collection ***War Zone***

I have recently published the e-chapbook *War Zone*. My poetry has appeared in the anthologies: *Genom Lövverket*, *Best of Paper Lanterns Anthology* vol. 1, and the *Per Diem Daily Haiku* feature on the THF website. I'm not very active in the haiku community anymore. The goals I once set up for myself have basically been realized. As a singer, you're always an interpreter of the words and music of someone else. Finding a new voice in haiku made me grow as a person and has also developed me as a singer. At the moment I'm working on a poetry collection in Swedish. It's a long term project and it will mostly contain free short verse, still very much influenced by haiku.

this side of winter
death speaks
in our mother tongue
bones 10

I reach
for the wind

only to feel
the nothingness

slip through
unpublished

the sea rests
and you rest in me

and the swallows reach
towards the sky
unpublished

a house in silence
only candle stumps left
of the night
Blåeld 3

his birth star

beyond
the heavy clouds

beyond
the burnt out cars
unpublished

deep in
my bones

sing no
more lies
NOON 12

Name Rebecca Lilly
Volume *A New Resonance* 2
Residence Port Republic VA
Occupation Writer / Photographer
Collections *Shadwell Hills*
A Prism of Wings
Yesterday's Footprints
Elements of a Life

I work as a writer, photographer, and field and office assistant to a landscape architect. I've earned degrees from Cornell (M.F.A., poetry) and Princeton (Ph.D., philosophy) Universities and have published several poetry collections, including two of haiku from Red Moon Press: Yesterday's Footprints and Elements of a Life. In addition, I have a letterpress book of haiku, Shadwell Hills (Birch Book Press), with original woodblock prints by Frank C. Eckmair. My website features selections from my photographic portfolio (primarily fruits and flowers) and offers purchase of notecards and gift enclosures based on those images.

Listening to snowfall . . .
the strange things
I can't explain about myself
Modern Haiku 37.3

Deepening snowfall . . .
a crow tightens its spiral
about the steeple
Snapshots 10

fine spring rain —
the jerk of a fishing line
through the river mist
Tundra 1

Only the cemetery
unchanged; vaguely,
remembering old ways
Modern Haiku 37.1

First snow —
the white mounds of snow
beside the closed station
Brussels Sprout 9.3

Autumn evening —
yellow leaves cover
the plot reserved for me
Modern Haiku 30.2

Name **Erik Linzbach**
Volume ***A New Resonance* 7**
Residence **Dewey AZ**
Occupation **Novelist**

No update.

rest home garden
tomatoes rotting
on the vine
Modern Haiku 44.2

unpicked orchard
her son's room
just as it was
Frogpond 36.2

two older girls
show me a trick
fresh cherries
Presence 49

softly scrambling eggs
she asks me
about my wife
Modern Haiku 45.2

watching her sleep
the gentle heave
of stormclouds
Modern Haiku 45.3

a well worn mattock
leans against the shed
autumn moonlight
Autumn Moon Haiku Contest
1st Place

Name **Burnell Lippy**
Volume ***A New Resonance* 1**
Residence **Burlington VT**
Occupation **Farmer**
Collection ***late geese up a dry fork***

No update.

> lily stamens
> almost touching
> cicada cry
> *The Heron's Nest* IV:9

> squash vines
> long and hollow
> the last late evenings
> *Frogpond* 25.3

> the twists
> in old coyote shit
> autumn wind
> *RAW NerVZ* X:3

> the end of a log
> still wet from a turtle —
> summer moon
> unpublished

> such a cold night
> the uneven stones
> of the walk
> unpublished

> winter rain —
> the shed's last firewood
> slips loose of its bark
> unpublished

Name **Chen-ou Liu**
Volume *A New Resonance 7*
Residence **Ajax Ontario**
Occupation **Freelance Writer**
Collections *Following the Moon to the Maple Land*
A Life in Transition and Translation

I am currently the editor and translator of *NeverEnding Story* and the author of five books, including *Following the Moon to the Maple Land* (First Prize, 2011 Haiku Pix Chapbook Contest) and *A Life in Transition and Translation* (Honorable Mention, 2014 Turtle Light Press Biennial Haiku Chapbook Competition). My tanka and haiku have been honored with 105 awards. I write haiku everyday, trying to catch a real frog in my imaginative lotus pond.

winter twilight
crossing the border
a child's shadow
<sub>New Zealand Poetry Society
Haiku Contest 2016, 4th Prize</sub>

cliff edge . . .
the sound of waiting
for nothing
<sub>New Zealand Poetry Society Haiku
Contest 2016, Highly Commended</sub>

distant sirens
over the border bridge
a blood moon
<sub>Touchstone Distinguished
Poem Award 2015, Shortlist</sub>

first glimpse
of her mastectomy bra
winter rose
<sub>Devidé Haiku Award 2015
Runner-Up</sub>

a monarch
folds into silence . . .
budding petals
<sub>World Haiku Competition 2014
Second Place</sub>

im-mi-grant . . .
the way English tastes
on my tongue
<sub>Kokako Haiku Competition 2013
Second Prize</sub>

Name: Gregory Longenecker
Volume: *A New Resonance* 9
Residence: Pasadena CA
Occupation: Retired
Collection: *somewhere inside yesterday*

I have received First Place awards in the 2017 H. Gene Murtha Memorial Senryu Contest and the 2017 Irish Haiku Society Haiku/Senryu Contest; Best of Issue, 2016 *Ershik: Journal of Senryu*; and Haiku of Merit in the 28th Ito En Haiku Contest. I have served as a judge for the 2016 HSA Haibun Contest and twice been Contest Chair for the Yuki Teikei Haiku Society's Tokutomi Haiku Contest. A new chapbook of my haiku, *somewhere inside yesterday*, has been released by Red Moon Press. I walk regularly in parks and gardens near my home, both for exercise and inspiration. I love to read mysteries, poetry and science fiction and with my wife, Renate, frequently attend movies. I write haiku daily, tanka and haibun less often. I make presentations to the Southern California Haiku Study Group from time to time and noodle around books and journals for new topics to present.

prayer book
all the funeral cards
but hers
Modern Haiku 48.3

childhood
the silence of God
on Sunday afternoons
Prune Juice 21

beneath the waves
the pearled words
of oysters
tinywords 17.1

stepfamily some assembly required
Mariposa 36

equinox
the weight
of dying light
Irish Haiku Society
Contest 2016, First Place

home from camp . . .
how much smaller
my parents seem
Frogpond 39.1

Name **Eve Luckring**
Volume *A New Resonance 6*
Residence Los Angeles CA
Occupation Visual Artist
Collections *fifty-three divided by seven or eight*
The Tender Between

Since appearing in *A New Resonance 6*, my poetry has been published in several anthologies and received awards both in the U.S. and Japan. In 2012, *antantantantant* published my first chapbook, *fifty-three divided by seven or eight*, as volume xiii of its online journal. *R'r* published an interview I conducted with translator and critic, Makoto Ueda, in Volumes 12.3 (2012) and 13.1 (2013). In 2015, I was honored to be interviewed by Michele Root-Bernstein for *Frogpond* 38.1 about the relationship between my video work and haiku. *The Tender Between*, my first book, was published in March 2018 with Ornithopter Press.

… *peace, but a sword.* cut the baby in half
   Modern Haiku 43.1

maybe in my amygdala maybe a minefield
   bones 4

rush hour
I enter
in third person
   The Heron's Nest XVI:1

< a cat
> a carcass
28 flies
   Modern Haiku 43.3

a beetle leg twitches golden the quiet
   Frogpond 38.3

until trees can be landlords
   The Heron's Nest XVII:2

Name   Bob Lucky
Volume *A New Resonance 6*
Residence   Jubail Saudi Arabia
Occupation Teacher
Collection *Ethiopian Times*

It's such a short "poem", but there are those who love it. As for my "career", I've been writing haiku in one form or another since the 5-7-5 days of elementary school. I've managed to publish a few, as well as a chapbook of haibun, *Ethiopian Times*. I'm currently the content editor at *Contemporary Haibun Online*. In addition to writing haiku and other forms, I spend a lot of time going back and forth between Saudi Arabia and northern Portugal, playing ukuleles and related stringed instruments, badly, and cooking . . . Well, perhaps more eating than cooking.

summer's end
the sparkle of coins
in the fountain
tinywords 17.2

Fourth of July
the dog that doesn't belong
to anyone
Modern Haiku 48.2

fading stars the stiffness of shadow puppets
Modern Haiku 47.2

waiting for death I miss the bus
A Hundred Gourds 5.2

raking leaves
the wind and I
take turns
Presence 48

boys killing a snake
because it's a snake —
dust devil
The Heron's Nest XVIII:2

Name	Scott Mason
Volume	*A New Resonance 6*
Residence	Chappaqua NY
Occupation	Branding Consultant
Collection	*The Wonder Code*

I'm the author of *The Wonder Code: Discover the Way of Haiku and See the World with New Eyes*, published in 2017. Since 2011 I've served as an editor with *The Heron's Nest*, and have co-judged the annual Haiku Society of America contests for senryu (with Alexis Rotella), haibun (with Penny Harter) and haiku (with Cor van den Heuvel). My own poems have won over 150 awards in international haiku competitions, including more than twenty first-place finishes. I believe that my haiku practice enables me to live my life with greater attentiveness, appreciation and joy. Besides haiku, my other passions include visiting art museums (harking back to my undergraduate major), engaging in active travel (including dozens of hiking and cycling trips on six continents to date) and hitting the golf course or beach.

epochs in the making
the box canyon's
sudden chill
The Wonder Code

unclipped forsythia
all children
can sing
The Wonder Code

the faint melody
of a carousel
swirling leaves
The Wonder Code

the sea lettuce
on my face mask
a late Matisse
The Wonder Code

her hoop earrings
tigers leaping
to mind
The Wonder Code

nocturne
the French horn soloist's
hidden hand
The Wonder Code

Name **Dan McCullough**
Volume ***A New Resonance* 3**
Residence **Arlington MA**
Occupation **Teacher Naturalist**

I've been fortunate to have haiku appear in publications including, *Modern Haiku, Frogpond, Bottle Rockets, Mayfly*, and *Acorn* between 2001 – 2009 and to have my work published in anthologies such as *A New Resonance* 3, *Montage*, and *Baseball Haiku: The Best Haiku Ever Written about the Game*. My job working for an Audubon Wildlife Sanctuary inspires my work as I'm able to slow down, focus, and become aware of the seasonal changes happening immediately around me and throughout New England. Though I continue to write various forms of poetry, I have opted not to submit my haiku anymore. Writing is a large part of who I am and I've enjoyed the times I've been able to interact with the haiku community.

stuck behind
the funeral procession
the parade twirlers
bottle rockets 16

catching
the first cherry petal
the caterpillar tent
Modern Haiku 37.3

barroom fight
unable to hear myself
drink
bottle rockets 18

lonely night
the frequent kiss
of a tequila worm
Modern Haiku 36.1

during
the pitching change
cicadas
Baseball Haiku

with or without
the telescope
the milky way
Modern Haiku 39.2

Name **Tanya McDonald**
Volume *A New Resonance 7*
Residence **Woodinville WA**
Occupation **Writer**
Collection *Seven Suns, Seven Moons*

Since my appearance in *A New Resonance 7*, I've been teaching haiku workshops for beginners at various venues, including the Seabeck Haiku Getaway, the Tacoma Poetry Festival, and even at a clothing boutique. In 2013, I was the regional coordinator for the Washington State region of the HSA, and I have since held the positions of president, secretary, and vice-president of Haiku Northwest (the Seattle-area haiku group). In 2014, I was a featured reader at the 25th annual Two Autumns Reading in San Francisco. That year, I also co-edited Haiku Northwest's 25th Anniversary Anthology, *No Longer Strangers*, which took 2nd place in the 2015 Kanterman Book Awards. 2016 saw the publication of *Seven Suns/ Seven Moons*, a quirky poetry collaboration with Michael Dylan Welch, and in 2017, I was the judge for the San Francisco International Rengay Competition, sponsored by the Haiku Poets of Northern California. I also write young adult fiction (nothing yet published) and longer form poetry. If I'm not at home drinking tea, watching birds, and writing, I'm likely at a bookstore or library. Or catching the bus into Seattle for haiku/fiction fodder. Or watching *Doctor Who* with my husband, Russell, who has put up with my writing shenanigans for over twenty years, and has even participated in a few of them.

hummingbird —
talk of building
a wall
Earthtones

fading suntan —
the pua-kenikeni blossoms
still fragrant
Acorn 38

Monday the warbler of my attention span
Mariposa 34

spring and all the darkness between Tube stations
Modern Haiku 46.3

skylight
boxing
the stars
Frogpond 37.2

garbage day —
blindsided
by morning honeysuckle
The Heron's Nest XVII:3

Name Joe McKeon
Volume *A New Resonance* 10
Residence Strongsville
Occupation Human Being

I continue to write poems on a daily basis. I have been recognized in international contests including the Robert Spiess Contest, the Harold G. Henderson contest, the Vancouver Cherry Blossom Contest, the Gene Murtha Senryu Contest, the Japanese Embassy (JICC) contest, The Hortensia Anderson contest and the "Three Rivers" Ivanić-Grad contest. Since *A New Resonance* 10 I have created a video chapbook entitled *Three Generations* that was presented at the Haiku North America conference in Santa Fe, New Mexico.

Ellis Island
my father winds
his father's watch
JICC Contest 2016
Grand Prize

flea market
we once had
it all
Gerald Brady Senryu Contest 2016
2nd Place

shelters full . . .
a bedtime story read
by moonlight
Mayfly 62

fifth floor walk-up
an elevated train screeches
through the heat
The Heron's Nest XIX:3

shades drawn
the sun slips in
under the door
Acorn 39

another year
the names of perennials
only she knew
Frogpond 40.2

Name **Jonathan McKeown**
Volume ***A New Resonance* 9**
Residence **Sydney Australia**
Occupation **Plumber**

I have had poems selected for inclusion in several anthologies including *Haiku 2014* (eds. Lee Gurga and Scott Metz), *Dust Devils: The Red Moon Anthology* 2016 (ed. Jim Kacian), and *They Gave Us Life: Celebrating Mothers and Fathers in Haiku* (ed. Robert Epstein). I have made some contributions to the Australian Haiku Society website, and was invited to write a review of *Journeys: An Anthology of International Haibun* (ed. Angelee Deodhar) which was published on *Contemporary Haibun Online*. I will be presenting a discussion paper on haiku at an upcoming meeting of The Poetic Injustice Society, a local poetry group based in Marrickville near where I live. I am currently working on a book of haibun. Since the publication of *A New Resonance 9* I have entered into the covenant of marriage with the lovely Els Van Leeuwen, another *New Resonance* haiku poet. We both work full time and seek to raise three children, as well as find time to write a poem or two in the midst of it all. Thankfully we have a beautiful little creek running through a bushland reserve near our house in Bardwell Valley where we can retreat from the stresses of city life.

morning fog
throwing a cricket
off its song
Modern Haiku 48.3

dead wood
the ministry
of wind
bottle rockets 32

deep rust where the analogy begins
bones 11

silica sparkles in stone cicadas
CHO 12.2

still warm
long after sundown
gravestone
Modern Haiku 48.2

woodsmoke
through moonlit trees
the light of a house
CHO 13.3

Name **Scott Metz**
Volume ***A New Resonance* 5**
Residence **South Beach OR**
Occupation **Public School Teacher**
Collections ***lakes & now wolves***
A Sealed Jar of Mustard Seeds

I'm the author of *lakes & now wolves* (Modern Haiku Press, 2012), and co-editor of *Haiku 21*, and the trilogy *Haiku 2014, 2015* and *2016* (Modern Haiku Press). I was one of the editors of R'r (aka *Roadrunner*) and I am the current editor of *is/let*.

the weight of a crow
perched naked
on a semi-colon
R'r 12.1

man
u
fact
u

red
rose

echoing mountain
lingering body

the river entering the
sea a sheet of
paper
NOON 8

Modern Haiku 44.2

BEHEADING

green light
is/let September 11, 2014

at the edge of the sea
a box of my teeth has found me
on a cold day
Modern Haiku 46.1

burning the money god a smaller one
otata 8

Name **paul m.**
Volume *A New Resonance 2*
Residence **Bristol RI**
Occupation **Financial Controller**
Collections *pilgrim stone*
Finding the Way
Called Home
Few Days North Days Few

paul m. is the pen name of Paul Miller, an internationally awarded and anthologized poet and essayist. Most recently I've won the British Haiku Society Haiku Award (2015) and Haiku Northwest's Francine Porad Award (2017). I've published three collections of haiku: *Finding the Way* (Press here, 2002), *Called Home* (Red Moon Press, 2006) and *Few Days North Days Few* (Red Moon Press, 2011); all of which have won a Haiku Society of America book award and the most recent a Haiku Foundation Touchstone Award. I served as treasurer of the Haiku Society of America (2004 – 2014) and Haiku Poets of Northern California (2003 –), and incorporated Haiku North America as a non-profit, currently serving as its CFO (2004 –). I served as book review editor of *Modern Haiku* (2005 – 2013) and since 2013 as managing editor.

grass trampled
by demonstrators
Earth Day
<small>Gerald Brady Senryu Contest 2015
1st Place</small>

becoming morning . . .
the hedge redirects
a dove's flight
<small>*Muttering Thunder 2*</small>

knee-high grass
a bison's slow rise
from the wallow
<small>*The Heron's Nest* XVI:3</small>

greening meadow . . .
a wood warbler sings
his grandfather's song
<small>*otata* 23</small>

winter gathering —
bits of bone too
heavy for the wind
<small>HPNC Haiku Contest 2015
1st Place</small>

Jasper John's *Flag* behind glass my museum voice
<small>*Mariposa* 29</small>

Name Fonda Bell Miller
Volume *A New Resonance 7*
Born 24 June 1947
Died 30 January 2017

Fonda Bell Miller was born 24June1947 in Greenville, North Carolina. For 18 years, she taught elementary school and reading recovery. She lived in Alexandria, Virginia, volunteered for the "Rock" kitchen, tutored for UCM, and was known as "an endlessly kind and nurturing soul who was devoted to her family and friends". She was a member of the Towpath Haiku Society for many years. Her first published haiku appeared in *Dragonfly* in 1982. Her work was published in *Modern Haiku*, *Frogpond*, *White Lotus*, *The Christian Science Monitor*, *Wisteria*, *Scifaikuest*, *moonset*, *Two Dragonflies*, *bottle rockets*, and others. Her tanka appeared in *moonbathing* and *Red Lights*, and her photo haiga in *Contemporary Haibun* and *Modern Haiga*.

picking tomatoes
on my hands the scent
of other summers
Modern Haiku 28.1

my old friend
her deep cough
autumn night
Frogpond 31.3

not yet day
snow making light
of darkness
The Haiku Calendar 2009

midnight star
how far away
the past
bottle rockets 23

nest song
and is it enough
little wren
A New Resonance 7

invisible now
the path I followed
river starlight
A New Resonance 7

Name **Andrea Missias**
Volume ***A New Resonance* 1**
Residence **Philadelphia PA**
Occupation **Social Activist**

No update.

    winter rain —
    the bright colors
    of the playground benches
        Frogpond 26.2

each carriage horse
resting one leg —
summer afternoon
   Modern Haiku 33.2

    three broken pots
    coming from that kiln
    and then that bowl
        black bough 12

sun through yellow leaves
the toddler swings his arms
above his head
   Frogpond 29.2

    silent train
    the man ahead of me also
    watches the darkness
        Persimmon II.2

city park —
the wind takes a leaf
from the chessboard
   Herb Barrett Haiku Contest 1998

Name: Ben Moeller-Gaa
Volume: A New Resonance 9
Residence: St Louis MO
Occupation: IT Senior Functional Analyst
Collections: *Wasp Shadows*
Blowing on a Hot Soup Spoon
Wishbones

My first full length collection of haiku, *Wishbones*, is due out in 2018 from Folded Word. I am also the author of two haiku chapbooks, the Pushcart nominated *Wasp Shadows* from Folded Word (2014) and *Blowing on a Hot Soup Spoon* from poor metaphor design (2014). I have the pleasure and honor to read, speak, mentor and do workshops around the St. Louis area both in schools and in the community. Haiku has made a big difference in my life. I'm so much more aware of everything around me. I just wanted to say a big "Thank You" to all of the other poets and editors out there who are active in journals and books. You continually teach me new tricks of the trade and help make this tiny genre such a wonderfully large and lively conversation across the globe!

weekday morning
pulling my mood
off a hanger
tinywords 17.2

winding to where
the river used to be
grandpa's story
Frozen Butterfly 2

evening calm
a spider webbing
the breeze
Shamrock 32

all day rain
the refrigerator's
ommmmm
Modern Haiku 46.3

catching my gaze
in the café window
autumn loneliness
Acorn 38

seaside café
the bottomless cup
of her story
Frogpond 38.1

Name **Beverly Acuff Momoi**
Volume *A New Resonance* 9
Residence **Mountain View CA**
Occupation **Writer**
Collection *Lifting the Towhee's Song*

In 2015, I was one of the featured readers at the Two Autumns reading sponsored by the Haiku Poets of Northern California. I presented at both HNA 2015 and HNA 2017 on haibun. In 2017 I was elected the 2nd Vice President of Haiku Society of America. My haiku are widely published in haiku journals and included in *Haiku 2015*; *galaxy of dust: Red Moon Press Anthology 2015*; *Earth in Sunrise: A Course for English-Language Haiku Study*; *The Wonder Code*; and Snapshot Press' *Haiku Calendar 2018*, as well as the upcoming *Women's Haiku Anthology*. My haibun collection, *Lifting the Towhee's Song*, was a Snapshot Press eChapbook Award winner. I live in northern California with my husband and two cats.

thin ice
the crackling sound
when she breathes
On Down the Road

saltgrass
quick to reveal
old hurts
earthsigns

out of the snow the outline of her voice
A Hundred Gourds 5.2

in the drought an unreliable narrator
Mariposa 33

my biggest fears
are nameless
moons of Jupiter
Modern Haiku 48.1

an inkling
of her backstory
rough-winged swallow
Acorn 34

Name Matt Morden
Volume *A New Resonance* 2
Residence Hermon Wales
Occupation Government Official
Collection *Stumbles in Clover*

No update.

winter solstice
a flock of starlings
takes a new shape
The Heron's Nest III:3

end of the holiday
a square of pale grass
beneath the tent
Acorn 3

summer's end
i stop myself talking
to a stranger's child
Presence 19

first day of spring
all the fly-fishing books
out of the library
unpublished

behind the tractor
a cloud of lime
becomes the valley mist
unpublished

friday evening
the chip shop counter
worn by small change
unpublished

Name	Ron C. Moss
Volume	*A New Resonance* 4
Residence	Leslie Vale Tasmania
Occupation	Digital Technician
Collections	*Ancient Bloodlines*
	Bushfire Moon
	The Bone Carver

I continue to write and share haiku and related genres and take part in the world community of haiku through various activities. These include judging various competitions like the Touchstone Book Awards and The Jane Reichhold Memorial Haiga competitions and the Australian Haiku Society seasonal kukai. My recent book collections have been well received and *The Bone Carver* won a Touchstone Distinguished Book Award (The Haiku Foundation) as well as a Merit Book Award Honourable Mention (Haiku Society of America). Also haiku awards: a Touchstone Individual Haiku Awards for "prenuptial contract" and shortlisted for "fire duty". My haiku has been included in several high profile anthologies: *Where the River Goes: The Nature Tradition in English-Language Haiku* and *Haiku In English: The First Hundred Years*. I have contributed art and design for many haiku related projects including all issues if the successful *A Hundred Gourds* online journal and *Nest Feathers*. My deep love continues for haiku and its wonderful community and the joy it brings in its many forms.

    old horses
    days of endless rain
    in their eyes
        The Heron's Nest XVI:4

fire duty
the newly ironed shirt
still warm
    The Heron's Nest XVI:1

morning frost . . .
sparks fly from the hands
of a knife maker
    NZPS International Haiku Competition 2017
    Commended

prenuptial contract
fish bones neatly spaced
on white china
    Acorn 30

    newborn lamb
    a first look towards
    the stars
        Presence 54

faraway rain
the chime of a nail
driven deeper
    The Heron's Nest XVIII:2
    Editor's Choice

Name H. Gene Murtha
Volume *A New Resonance 6*
Born 19 October 1955
Died 9 October 2015
Collections *Memorial Day*
Biding Time

H. Gene Murtha, poet and naturalist, was born in Philadelphia, Pennsylvania. He served as tanka editor of a short form poetry online publication *Notes from the Gean* and was a member of The Haiku Society of America, The Tanka Society of America, Haiku Oz, the Pennsylvania Poetry Society, Mad Poets Society, and The Nick Virgilio Haiku Association. He sponsored and judged the first haiku contest for the inner city children of Camden, New Jersey for the Virgilio Group. Murtha's work was included in *Haiku in English: The First Hundred Years* [edited by Jim Kacian, Philip Rowland, and Allan Burns] (W.W. Norton and Company, 2013). He was one of seventeen poets featured in *A New Resonance 6: Emerging Voices in English-Language Haiku* (Red Moon Press, 2009). Some of his awards include: Readers Choice Award, *White Lotus 3* (2006); Special Mention, *The Heron's Nest* Valentine Award (2003); Special Mention, *The Heron's Nest* Valentine Award (2006); and Runner-up, Innovative Category, *HaikuNow!* (The Haiku Foundation, 2010).

first warm day
a robin works
the infield
The Heron's Nest XVII:3

summer haze —
a crow flaps free
of the asphalt
Frogpond 27.1

when you think
you've heard it all —
brown thrasher
The Heron's Nest XI:4

morning chill
a child's shadow
moves thru mine
A New Resonance 6

Berlin Wall
a smooth stone
in my pocket
Haiku in English

spring mist —
a mallard paddles
through our stillborn's ashes
Memorial Day

Name: Pamela Miller Ness
Volume: *A New Resonance 2*
Residence: New York NY
Occupation: Learning Specialist
Collections: *Limbs of the Gingko*
A Thousand Paper Cranes
Alzheimer's Waltz
Driveway from Childhood

I have served the Haiku Society of America in many capacities, including President 2006–2007. I served as editor of the *Tanka Society of America Newsletter* from 2000–2003 and chaired the organizing committee for Haiku North America New York City, June 2003. My paper "Prosody in Haiku," presented at HNA 2005, was subsequently published in *Modern Haiku* and anthologized in the 2006 *Red Moon Anthology*. In 2005, I founded *red lights*, a semi-annual journal devoted to English-language tanka. I edited *The Tanka Anthology* (with Michael McClintock and Jim Kacian), and my other collections include *the hole in Buddha's heel*, *Like Salt on Sun Spray, a new arrangement*, *the hands of women*, *pink light, sleeping*, and *Scent of Jasmine and Brine*.

after all these years
ankle deep
in the other ocean
Frogpond 21.2

new year's rain
the circles in the puddle
widen
The Haiku Calendar 2000 Winner

deathwatch
I braid my hair
a little tighter
Bashō Festival Anthology 2002

after chemo
wanting only to read
seed catalogues
Acorn 2

spotlit room
the chip
in Buddha's chin
bottle rockets 1

Christmas eve —
the row of cut trees
no one took home
Modern Haiku 29.2

Name: Peter Newton
Volume: *A New Resonance* 8
Residence: Winchendon MA
Occupation: Stained Glass Artist
Collections: *What We Find*
Welcome to the Joy Ride
A Path of Desire
The Searchable Word

Like the literary form of haiku my life is deceptively simple. I continue to write each morning for as long as I have something to say. Sometimes, no writing occurs. When the times comes I walk to an old barn behind my house where I earn a living as a stained glass artist. I work with my hands assembling things almost like writing a poem. The haiku come to me in fits and starts. Here and there. And gradually along the way. I find the challenge of writing haiku to be writing one that hasn't been written before. To this end I try to keep open to the world and to read more. Not only haiku but books of all types. Currently, the consciousness of octopuses and a compendium of rare and endangered words are among the topics on my nightstand. I visit my local library as a kind of field trip during the work week. Since I tend to write "in a bubble" so to speak I enjoy the company of other poets when that happens. I enjoy co-editing the online journal *tinywords* and the many conversations at the annual Haiku Circle gathering in Northfield, MA. Of course, Twitter is its own kind of literary minefield but can sometimes surprise you. (@ThePeterNewton)

over the crib
a universe
in suspense
Frogpond 40.1

snow globe
the perfect day
to stay inside
otata 15

impossibly the orchid pulling off its blue
bones 13

river swim clearing the headlines
Acorn 37

casket
the matte black finish
of his first car
Modern Haiku 46.2

headlong off the jetty
when I was
a superhero
The Heron's Nest XVIII:4

Name **Christina Nguyen**
Volume ***A New Resonance* 8**
Residence **Hugo MN**
Occupation **Copywriter**

art house films
my life before
I had kids
tinywords 14.1

magnolia blossoms
his hands move
to the deep south
VerseWrights 31 October 2014

what I thought   polar vortex   what is
Red Dragonfly 9 March 2014

that being said a crow over morning coffee
bones 4

inside
the biodegradable bag
a disposable diaper
Prune Juice 17

so many nightmares
this tangle of cables
next to my bed
tinywords 17.2

Name Polona Oblak
Volume *A New Resonance* 9
Residence Ljubljana Slovenia
Occupation Senior Bank Officer

My work is regularly published in major print and on line journals and several of my haiku have placed in contests. My haiku appeared in anthologies like *Nest Feathers, Haiku 2015, A Vast Sky, Naad Anunad, The Wonder Code*, and a number of volumes of *The Red Moon Anthology* (2006, 2011, 2012, 2013, 2015, 2016, 2017) and I have haiku accepted to appear in *Women's Haiku Anthology*. Since 2015 I have served as assistant editor at *tinywords*. I'm an introvert living and working in Ljubljana, Slovenia. I have spent over 30 years dealing with other people's (or, rather, institutions') money. Having had no previous affinity for creative writing I came across haiku around the beginning of 2005 and knew instantly this was something I could do and would like to continue doing. It has turned out to be a long-term commitment.

the oven glove's
blackened thumb...
winter lingers

Modern Haiku 47.1

slow thunder
the lizard's ribs pressed
against concrete

The Heron's Nest XVIII:2

workday's end
the shifting pink
of petals

Vancouver Cherry Blossom
Haiku Contest 2015, Sakura Award

something limp
in a kestrel's talons
afternoon moon

Acorn 38

heat lightning
something ancient
in a lizard's eye

The Heron's Nest XIX:3

record heat
the olm's gills flutter pink
in a cave pool

Frogpond 40.3

Name **Fumio Ogoshi**
Volume ***A New Resonance* 1**
Residence **Irvine CA**
Occupation **Computer Programmer**

No update.

    spring bloom —
    a young girl singing
    beyond her range
        A New Resonance 1

a school of fish
following the clouds —
coolness
   A New Resonance 1

    peeling an orange —
    the sourness
    before the taste
        A New Resonance 1

after the story —
a slow cough, cough
for an ending
   A New Resonance 1

    a broken flower pot —
    sunlight leaking
    through the cracks
        A New Resonance 1

lost child —
clinging onto the legs
of a mannequin
   A New Resonance 1

Name: Renée Owen
Volume: *A New Resonance 7*
Residence: Sebastopol CA
Occupation: Psychotherapist
Collection: *Alone on a Wild Coast*

The haiku path continues to enrich my life, keeping me attuned to the present moment. Publishing is a rewarding way to share my work with others, and the related deadlines are a great motivator. My collection of haiku and haibun, *Alone on a Wild Coast* (Snapshot Press), received an Honorable Mention in the 2014 Touchstone Distinguished Book Awards. I edited *Scent of the Past... Imperfect* (Two Autumns Press), an Honorable Mention recipient in HSA's 2017 Merit Book Awards, and continue to publish internationally in journals & anthologies. Recent awards include placing in the HSA Haiku and Haibun Contests, CVHC's Kilbride Haibun Contest, and the SF International Rengay Competition. The camaraderie of fellow poets along the way enlivens my journey, like serving on The Haiku Foundation's Touchstone Awards' juror panel, and as Hospitality Chair for the Haiku Poets of Northern California. I enjoy performing my poetry with my musician husband, who accompanies me at readings on shakuhachi, guitar, mandolin and harmonica. In addition to my work as a psychotherapist, I love creating and exhibiting book and fiber art. A passion for the environment and sustainability inspires my creative process, and fragments of poems weave their way into my art. Weekends, I can be found hiking the wilds near our Northern California home.

rising seas
a single shorebird
in last light
Acorn 39

indigo night
this star-studded sky
for my shroud
Frogpond 40.2

a trunk here
leaves there
oak gall ink
Frogpond 40.1

the susurration
of wet cedar trees
restless night
Acorn 38

a lone coyote—
all that's keeping me
in check
Mariposa 34

a steady stream
of fences
refugee moon
Modern Haiku 48.2

Name **w f owen**
Volume ***A New Resonance 2***
Residence **Antelope CA**
Occupation **Professor of Communications**
Collections ***small events***
small events ebook

I was educated at the University of Hawaii at Manoa, specializing in speech and English education, and at the University of Washington in Seattle, Washington, where I received a PhD in Speech Communication in 1982. My main teaching interests include interpersonal communication and the role of artistic communication in personal development. I've published haiku, senryu and haibun in such journals as *Frogpond, Modern Haiku, Acorn, bottle rockets, Mayfly* and *Contemporary Haibun*. I was a featured reader at the 2003 Haiku Poets of Northern California's Two Autumns Reading and edited the Two Autumns chapbook *If I Met Bashô* in 2005. As President of the Central Valley Haiku Club (California), I co-edited the club's three chapbooks: *blink, feel of the handrail,* and *Tangled in Dreams*. I also served as Haibun Editor for the online journal *Simply Haiku* for two years.

Indian summer
a spent salmon
washes ashore
*Henderson Haiku Contest 2004
First Place*

another argument unfolds the futon
bottle rockets 4

aftershock
the picture on the wall
straightens
*Brady Senryu Contest 2003
First Place*

cold front
the honey jar releases
its lid
Acorn 5

on the bank
fish holding the curve
of the bucket
Frogpond 25.1

Indian summer
a fish slips through
the gill net
*Henderson Haiku Contest 2004
Third Place*

Name **Roland Packer**
Volume *A New Resonance* 6
Residence **Hamilton Ontario**
Occupation **Musician**
Collection *Wayfarers*

After 2009 I started to submit regularly to haiku periodicals as well as receiving first place in both the 2012 British and 2013 San Francisco Haiku Competitions. In 2013 *in the shade of new leaves*, a Haiku Canada Sheet with a selection of my work was published (edited by LeRoy Gorman) and later a minichapbook, *Wayfarers*, was published by Phafours Press in 2017 (edited by Pearl Pirie).

leaving
the wayfarers' chapel
moonlight
tinywords 16.1

styx and bones the cry of a stone
Frogpond 36.3

to
tem
y
our
s
tor
y
be
come
s
mine

Goldilocks zone
I
of the storm
is/let 2016

evening breeze
through the barnboards
final bid
Henderson Haiku Contest 2016
Honorable Mention

Modern Haiku 46.3

Name Tom Painting
Volume *A New Resonance 2*
Residence Atlanta GA
Occupation Creative Literature Teacher
Collection *Piano Practice*

Some highlights: I was a Workshop Presenter at Haiku North America in Santa Fe, NM in 2017. My book, Piano Practice, by Tom Painting (Bottle Rockets Press, 2004) took 3rd place in the HSA Merit Book Contest. I placed first in the HSA Haibun Contest 2012 and the Brady Senryu Contest in 2016. My haiku have been included in *Haiku in English: The First Hundred Years* (W. W. Norton, 2013) and *Baseball Haiku: The Best Haiku Ever Written About the Game* (W. W. Norton, 2007). My passions include my wife and kids, hiking, birdwatching, haiku. And I'm relearning the guitar after a 40-year absence.

spring plowing
a flock of blackbirds
turns inside out
Frogpond 25.2

first crocus
I make a promise
I can't keep
Shiki Kukai February 2007

detour
she returns my hand
to the wheel
Frogpond 26.3

summer stars
my children ask me
to name a favorite
The Heron's Nest XIII:2

forsythia
I forget the rest
of the story
Acorn 29

snowmelt
the cascading notes
of a canyon wren
Modern Haiku 46.1

Name **Brent Partridge**
Volume *A New Resonance* 1
Residence **Orinda CA**
Occupation **Garden Shop Worker**
Collection *The Wizard's Rook*

Fortunate enough not to need further fame, I don't enter poetry contests. In 1989 I began helping Takada Sakuzō with his translations of contemporary Japanese haiku: we translated about eight thousand, including many by Matsuzawa Akira, and by Iida Saburō. Takada-san found me a job in rural Japan, where I taught English and team-translated Shinto scriptures from 1994 to 1996. I live alone and completely off the grid. I grow lots of flowers — cut, arrange and give them away. At work, I'm able to teach a lot about gardening. It's been many years since I've done any translation work.

heron also
leaving the coast
carrying some of it
Frogpond 37.1

leaves light green —
the mourning dove on and on
yet not the whole song
Modern Haiku 47.3

cloud dragon
eating its own tail —
Epiphany Day
The Heron's Nest XVIII:2

laughter in the zendo —
guest students
tatami turning
bottle rockets 34

azure sky
through bare branches
included in the bouquet
Frogpond 35.1

turning from the breeze
in order to whistle
wildflowers
Modern Haiku 44.3

Name **Christopher Patchel**
Volume *A New Resonance* 3
Residence **Green Oaks IL**
Occupation **Graphic Designer**
Collection *Turn Turn*

My book, *Turn Turn*, was a 2013 Touchstone Award finalist, and the reviews it received in *Frogpond* and *Modern Haiku* were very gratifying (though it sold few copies). I've been doing the *Frogpond* covers since 2012. The exacting nature of the photo-art has been quite challenging but the responses from readers have made it worthwhile. I've also been in the *Frogpond* editor's chair since the end of 2016. Though I'd hoped to continue, the combination of these volunteer roles has proven to be full time work and therefore unsustainable, so I'll be stepping down as editor. I'm hoping that *Frogpond* will continue to thrive, and that creative excellence will remain a hallmark of the journal.

thrush notes
the play of light
on my eyelids
Acorn 20

slant light . . .
to each leaf
it's own fall
Acorn 20

Vivaldi my doodles
The Heron's Nest XVII:2

we turn turn our clocks ahead
HaikuNow! Contest 2011

fall colors . . .
believing I'll prove
the exception
Frogpond 37.1

best ofs
and worst ofs
another orbit
The Heron's Nest XVIII:3

Name Carl Patrick
Volume *A New Resonance* 1
Residence Brooklyn NY
Occupation English Professor

I have lived a quiet life in haiku. Conferences, contests, anthologies, public readings — yeah, I've been there. Mostly however, I have sat quietly on the margins of the haiku world trying endlessly to polish three lines. Basho has something about turning over a haiku ten thousand times on the tongue. And to think I took it up to become more spontaneous. I am nearly there. Thirty-five years of haiku, thousands of them, neatly sorted into a dozen unpublished collections. I stand timidly at the door of a publisher.

snow
falls on the lighthouse
in the snowglobe
Suspiciously Small

left atop
the family Bible
a flyswatter
Low Growling from the Petunias

its glittering lures
daddy's tackle box
open in my mind
A Gust from the Alley

shimmering on
a classroom ceiling
puddle of spring rain
unpublished

through the snow
warmth of the pizza box
on each palm
unpublished

on a quiet street
strolling side by side
the lady cigar smokers
unpublished

Name **Paul Pfleuger Jr.**
Volume ***A New Resonance* 4**
Residence **Chiayi Taiwan**
Occupation **English Teacher**
Collection ***a Zodiac***

I've served as Assistant Editor at *Roadrunner*, as a Haiku Foundation Feature Editor (with Jack Galmitz) on *Per Diem: Daily Haiku* and with the translation staff at the World Haiku Association. My awards include *The Heron's Nest* Award for issue VI:7; Second Prize in the The Kusamakura International Haiku Competition 2005; the Judge's Award in the 18th ITO EN Oi Ocha New Haiku Contest 2007; Second Place in the International Section of the 10th *Mainichi* Haiku Contest 2007; and the Scorpion Award from *Roadrunner* VIII:2.

calm night
each piglet
on a nipple
Acorn 15

dusting off a trail map:
the edge
of winter
Kusamakura Haiku Contest 2005
Second Prize

with you
at the back of my tongue —
the East River
Roadrunner VI:3

spring again —
a taste of rust
in the harmonica
The Heron's Nest VI:4

discussing divorce
the boy wants to adopt
an eagle
Haiku World December 2002

knowing all the words
to the song I hate —
summer's end
unpublished

Name: Stella Pierides
Volume: *A New Resonance* 10
Residence: London / Neusass
Occupation: Poet and Writer
Collections: *Of This World*
In the Garden of Absence
Feeding the Doves
Ekphrasis

My work has appeared in numerous journals and anthologies, most recently in *Old Song: The Red Moon Anthology of English-Language Haiku* 2017 (Red Moon Press, 2018); *Jumble Box* (Press Here, 2017); and received First Prize in the Sharpening The Green Pencil Haiku Contest 2017. I received a Merit Book Award in 2013; was included in *Haiku* 2014 (Modern Haiku Press), and in the European Top 100 most creative haiku authors for six consecutive years (2012 – 2017). I received an Honorable Mention in the International Sakura Awards (2015), Third Prize in the Kusamakura Haiku Competition (2014), amongst others. Besides my creative writing, articles include "Haiku and the brain: an exploratory study" (*Juxtapositions* 3.1) and "Reading English-language haiku: processes of meaning construction revealed by eye movements" (*JEMR*, 10.1). Currently, I manage the *Per Diem: Daily Haiku* feature for The Haiku Foundation and serve on the Foundation's board of directors. Recently, I served as a judge for the British Haiku Society's Haibun Contest 2017. I enjoy reading, gardening, film, music, food and walking. I am currently learning the practice of Yang Chengfu Tai Chi.

old photos
the dust never
settles
Of This World

carmine lipstick
and the swirl of her skirt . . .
first party
Ekphrasis: Between Image and Word

waiting room
how blossom turns
to fruit
Blithe Spirit 27.2

winter wind
the last leaf now
on top of the pile
Jumble Box

refugee child —
folding and unfolding
his paper boat
Sharpening the Green Pencil
Contest 2017, 1st Prize

wild stream
my thoughts
etc.
Kusamakura Haiku Contest 2017
3rd Prize

Name: **Gregory Piko**
Volume: ***A New Resonance 7***
Residence: **Yass NSW Australia**
Occupation: **Retired**
Collection: ***Blowing Up Balloons***

Gregory's haiku received a Touchstone Award from The Haiku Foundation (USA), won first prize in the New Zealand Poetry Society's international haiku competition and have appeared in a number of major anthologies including *Haiku in English: The First Hundred Years*. Gregory was Secretary of the Australian Haiku Society 2010 – 2014. More recently, he collaborated with Vanessa Proctor in writing *Blowing Up Balloons: baby poems for parents* (Red Moon Press, 2017). Gregory began writing haiku and related forms of poetry around 2002. Since 2010, he has also been writing free verse poetry which has appeared in Australian and USA journals and anthologies. His free verse poetry was included in *The Best Australian Poems* 2012 and was joint winner of the WB Yeats Poetry Prize for Australia. It also appeared in *Yeats 150: William Butler Yeats 1865 – 1939* (Lilliput Press, 2015).

rosebud
let's fall in love
once a year
bottle rockets 26

her cotton skirt
falls softly to the ground
steady rain
Presence 53

persimmons
well maybe this is
about Shiki
Kokako 24

a fishing village
fixed to the shoreline
Gaudi's mosaic
Modern Haiku 44.2

strung
between two kookaburras
the shine of a skink
The Heron's Nest XVIII:4

each petal
touching its neighbour
open garden
Modern Haiku 48.1

Name **Thomas Powell**
Volume ***A New Resonance* 9**
Residence **Gilford Northern Ireland**
Occupation **Pottery Business Owner**
Collection ***A Dawn of Ghosts***

I came across haiku in 2008 and was so enthralled by the form that I immediately set out to write my own versions. *A Dawn of Ghosts*, my first eChapbook was published by Snapshot Press in 2017.

honeysuckle the scent of summer passing
Shamrock Haiku 38

digging up thistles
deep into dusk
the white-haired farmer
Wild Plum 3.2

glacial erratic:
a sea breeze lifts
the stonechat
Blithe Spirit 26.1

freezing fog
a dog barks from where
the fox was heading
A Hundred Gourds 4.3

the finest rain
softly amongst spruce
the blackbird's subsong
Presence 60

where the air was sweet rotting haws
Chrysanthemum 17

Name **Vanessa Proctor**
Volume *A New Resonance* 3
Residence Sydney Australia
Occupation Editor / English Teacher
Collections *Temples of Angkor*
Jacaranda Baby
Blowing Up Balloons

I have been President of the Australian Haiku Society since 2016. I lead the Sydney-based haiku group, the Red Dragonflies, and am a member of the online haiku group Zazen which I co-founded in 1999. My publications include the chapbook *Temples of Angkor* (Sunline Press, 2003), the eChapbook *Jacaranda Baby* (Snapshot Press, 2012) and *Blowing Up Balloons: baby poems for parents* co-written with Gregory Piko (Red Moon Press, 2017). I was overall winner in the 2014 New Zealand Poetry Society International Haiku Competition and was a winner in the Snapshot Press Haiku Calendar Competition in 2011 and 2017. I judged the New Zealand Poetry Society's Junior Haiku Competition in 2012, the Martin Lucas Haiku Award in 2016 and was a judge for the British Haiku Society Haiku Award in 2017. In 2010 my haiku "night kayaking" was inscribed on a boulder on the Katikati Haiku Pathway in New Zealand. My haiku appear on tea bag tags in the Love and New Parent ranges of tea from the Australian-based company Monji Tea. As well as promoting the writing of haiku among adults, I have been encouraging young people to write haiku, working with a local Cub and Scout pack, as well as with my own children, who will hopefully form the next generation of haiku poets.

a trip to the park
again we stop at the place
where he lost his balloon
Blowing Up Balloons

the shortest day
hunting for fossils
on a pebble beach
Presence 55

all that I am mountain spring
NZ International Haiku Competition 2014 Overall Winner

sharpness of a winter's day gathering fallen limes
FreeExpresSion Haiku Competition 2014 2nd Place

dementia
the skywriting
just drifts away
Kokako 22

news of war
the red welt of a tick bite
slowly spreads
IAFOR Vladimir Devidé Haiku Contest 2015 Runner-Up

Name William Ramsey
Volume *A New Resonance* 2
Residence Myrtle Beach SC
Occupation Retired Professor
Collections *Good Wine*
More Wine
This Wine
Ascend with Care

After my second haiku book, *More Wine* (Red Moon Press, 2010), I gave up haiku writing, being creatively emptied. Also, chronic health issues further depleted me of available energy. Yet, in the last year, with an upturn in health I have resumed writing—haiku's special moment of creative lift has returned After my long break, returning to haiku gave me a new, blank slate—a fresh start to go in new directions and depart from past work and themes. Quite nice, frankly.

seeing just now
the width of this cosmos

a wolf howls

bones 12

what destination
can we ever reach?

my circling goldfish

bottle rockets 37

brushing new oils
into my landscape sky —

to improve heaven

Frogpond 40.3

this leaf on my palm —
genetic code for a great
maple forest

Hedgerow 120

trembling in the gusts
this weed's tiny flower
I've not seen before

Frogpond 40.2

staring at the moon
my dog the wolf
I the monkey

Modern Haiku 48.3

Name **Andrew Riutta**
Volume ***A New Resonance* 5**
Residence **Gaylord MI**
Occupation **Chef**

Around 1993, a co-worker introduced me to the author Jim Harrison. He became my obsession — then till now. In 1996, he published a book titled *After Ikkyu*. This book led me down the road to Asian poetry, haiku in particular: Bashō, Issa and Shiki. Santōka. Then tanka came along. These forms taught me, more than anything, that saying less is saying more. Crisp, sharp word usage. But also risk taking. Since the journey began, I've had a wonderful ride, which I believe I owe to the wonder of haiku. And tanka. My contemporaries helped fuel this joy and I've made some wonderful friends along the way. Love and miss ya H. Gene. I took a break from these forms for a few years. A breath of fresh air, I suppose; though I still occassionaly wrote. In 2016 I opened my own food trailer in northern Michigan called "the green onion: Asian-inspired dishes. Put down the pen for a pair of tongs. But now I feel the bones leaning, once again, toward this beautiful and sometimes dark chunk of land known as haiku. The heart of my world is forever my daughter, Issa. Seventeen years I have known her and each day I still get butterflies. I believe this feeling is what haiku attempts to capture and preserve. She is the poem I've wanted to write for most of my life.

AA meeting . . .
spring peepers lengthen
the moment of silence
South by Southeast 15.3

white lilacs
on a damp windowsill —
mother in diapers
Beyond Forgetting

autumn wind —
mother stares
where I cannot see
Beyond Forgetting

folded in prayer
my hands make
one big fist
Simply Haiku 2010

crows —
the dead suddenly
more dead
Under the Basho Spring 2018

Name: Chad Lee Robinson
Volume: *A New Resonance* 4
Residence: Pierre SD
Occupation: Grocery Store Manager
Collections: *Pop Bottles*
Rope Marks
The Deep End of the Sky

I began writing haiku in 2002. Since then I have published three contest-winning collections: *Pop Bottles* (True Vine Press, 2009), *Rope Marks* (Snapshot Press, 2012), and *The Deep End of the Sky* (Turtle Light Press, 2015) which also placed second in the Haiku Society of America's Merit Book Awards. My work has received many awards, including a *Modern Haiku* Award for senryu, a Pushcart Prize nomination from *Modern Haiku*, a Readers Choice Poem of the Year award from *The Heron's Nest*, and a Touchstone Award for Individual Poems. Notable anthology appearances include *Baseball Haiku* (W.W. Norton, 2007), *Haiku in English* (W.W. Norton, 2013), *Haiku 21* (Modern Haiku Press, 2011), 14 editions of the *Red Moon Anthology*, *Montage: The Book* (The Haiku Foundation, 2010), and *Nest Feathers: Selected Haiku from the First 15 Years of The Heron's Nest* (2015). I served as regional coordinator for the Plains & Mountains region of the Haiku Society of America from 2006–2011 and again in 2014. I served as a judge for The Haiku Foundation's Touchstone Book Awards from 2013–2015. I grew up in central South Dakota, along the banks of the Missouri River. I love the landscape of South Dakota, from its plains and rolling hills to its mountains. I get to share it all with my wife and my son.

one of the wolves
shows its face
firelight
South by Southeast XIX:3

spinning free
of the trick roper's lasso
dust devil
bottle rockets 30

prairie storm
the darkness disperses
as buffalo
The Heron's Nest XIX:3

until
I am earth again
rain moving through the bluestem
Acorn 30

tapping trail dust
from the harmonica . . .
twilight stars
tinywords 14.2

restringing fence wire —
the meadowlark's song one post
ahead of the wind
Mariposa 35

Name	Carolyne Rohrig
Volume	*A New Resonance* 1
Residence	Fremont CA
Occupation	Volunteer Coordinator
Collections	*Chalk Drawings* *Slicing the Morning Mist*

I am a participant in the haiku community in San Francisco. Over the years I've had my work published in the USA, Canada, Ireland, England and Japan. I coordinate the Haiku Poets of Northern California's yearly international competition, which gives me the joy of reading poets' entries and recruiting poets as judges for the competition. My work is frequently featured in HPNC's *Mariposa*. I sometimes have my work in anthologies, and last year my first chapbook *Slicing the Morning Mist* was published by Michael Ketchek's Free Food Press. When I'm not writing haiku, I'm painting and writing a memoir with my sister about growing up in three cultures.

scrambled eggs
I was never one
for boundaries
Slicing the Morning Mist

estate sale
discarding more
than I bargained for
Slicing the Morning Mist

bon voyage
a child's drawing off the page
onto the dog
Mariposa 37

new kitchen
old husband
wine with everything
Mariposa 36

my prescription
never running out
of days
Mariposa 31

humid day
the price for my silence
just went up
Mariposa 30

Name **Michele Root-Bernstein**
Volume *A New Resonance 6*
Residence East Lansing MI
Occupation Independent Scholar
Collection *The Haiku Life*

I've published haiku, haibun and haiga in English-language journals and anthologies, placed a number of times in prominent haiku, senryu and haibun contests, and judged one or two others. In addition to my *New Resonance 6* selection of haiku, I appear in *Scent of the Past . . . Imperfect* (Two Autumns Press, 2016). And three of my poems feature on rocks stationed along a beautiful haiku walk in Ohio. I served as associate editor of *Frogpond*, 2012–2015. In 2017, I co-authored *The Haiku Life, What We Learned as Editors of Frogpond* (Modern Haiku Press) with Francine Banwarth. Since spring 2016, I've facilitated the monthly Evergreen Haiku Study Group at the Center for Poetry, Michigan State University. When I am not reading or writing or teaching haiku, I spend my time exploring creative imagination from childhood to adulthood across the arts and sciences. I focus on haiku practice in interviews with several poets and in two essays: "Copying to Create: The Role of Imitation and Emulation in Developing Haiku Craft," (*Modern Haiku* 48.1) and "Haiku as Emblem of Creative Discovery: Another Path to Craft," (*Modern Haiku* 41.3).

one season following another Möbius strip tease
Haiku Canada Review 9.1

crickets altering pitch dark
Modern Haiku 48.3

the daisy's odds
and evens out
Frogpond 40.2

after the jackhammer
the hole
a hummingbird makes
Mariposa 33

every once
in a blue funk
moon
Mariposa 33

this morning
it takes the iris to open
forever
Acorn 31

Dave Russo (*A New Resonance* 5) elected not to participate in *Echoes* 2.

Name **Dan Schwerin**
Volume *A New Resonance* 8
Residence **Greendale WI**
Occupation **United Methodist Minister**
Collection *ORS*

Since my appearance in *A New Resonance* 8, I am grateful to have become a grandfather and to have a first collection published by Red Moon Press. I have been included in several journals and anthologies, including *Something Out of Nothing*, by Ion Codrescu, *Haiku 2014, 2015, 2016* by Gurga and Metz, the *Red Moon Anthologies* for 2013, 2014, and 2016, *The Haiku Life* by Root-Bernstein and Banwarth, and *The Wonder Code* by Scott Mason. My first collection, *ORS*, was published in 2015 and received a Touchstone Award for distinguished books. I enjoy the uproarious fun and learning in the monthly meetings of Haiku Waukesha — and would invite you to stop in soon.

the same porch light
part of you
summer evening
Modern Haiku 48.3

eggs in a shirt
to be here
so lightly
Frogpond 40.1

having othered others here for the blood of grapes
bones 12

they keep throwing more in the soup kitchen river
is/leet 8 April 2017

vacation or not
the biting fly
needs pastor
Modern Haiku 47.3

standing water
trying to be
something else
Frogpond 38.1

Name **Rob Scott**
Volume *A New Resonance* 10
Residence **Melbourne Australia**
Occupation **Teacher**
Collections *Out of Nowhere*
Down to the Wire

After writing haiku for almost 20 years, I released my first two major collections, *Out of Nowhere* and *Down to the Wire*, both published by Red Moon Press (2016). My haiku have been included the *Red Moon Anthologies* in 2001 – 04, 2006 and 2009, in addition to *Haiku 2016*, *Haiku 2015* and *Haiku 21* (Modern Haiku Press). My haiku have been widely published in print and online journals around the globe over the past 20 years and have won or received commendations in several competitions including Winner, Haiku Presence Award (2003), and Winner, Haiku Calendar Competition (Snapshot Press, 2002). In 2014, I completed a Master's thesis entitled *The History of Australian Haiku and the Emergence of a Local Accent*. In May 2015, I presented a paper on my findings at the Second International Haiku Conference in Krakow, entitled *Australian Haiku — Is it a Thing?* I was one of the judges in the Haiku Dreaming Australia Award (2009). A big sports fan, under the guise of "Haiku Bob", I have written a match report in haiku for every game my beloved Australian football team, the Collingwood Magpies, has played since 2007. I am a teacher who has worked in schools in Australia, Japan, Sweden and The Netherlands. My family and I have recently decided to return to Australia after living overseas for much of the last 20 years. I look forward to spending more time watching footy and walking along Elwood beach.

spicing up the stew —
she hands me coriander
in that dress
failed haiku 15

first snowflakes —
my grey hair surrounds
the barber's chair
Sonic Boom 5

mercury drops I get the cold shoulder
Sonic Boom 5

halfway through my news her soft snores
failed haiku 15

first snowflakes —
making light
of everything
Modern Haiku 46.2

peace rally —
my kids fight
over a balloon
prune juice 22

Name David Serjeant
Volume *A New Resonance* 10
Residence Chesterfield England
Occupation Government Officer
Collection *Smithereens*

No update.

spring breeze —
somewhere in the valley
playtime
Presence 40

school fair —
a trace of smoke
on the fire engine
Simply Haiku 6.4

talk of redundancies
spring bulbs emerge
in corporate colours
Smithereens

my colleague
flirting with the workman
endless summer rain
Riverbed 3

lost in thought
a breeze I can't feel
glows the embers
Shamrock 16

a late spring
the blackbird tries
a different song
Blithe Spirit 20.2

Name **Shloka Shankar**
Volume *A New Resonance* 10
Residence **Bangalore India**
Occupation **Freelance Writer/Editor**

I thought I was writing "haikus" like everyone else till I was introduced to the world of non-5-7-5 untitled poems! I became a member of the Facebook group *IN Haiku*, moderated by Kala Ramesh, in December 2013. It gave me the golden opportunity to workshop my poems and learn by reading the works of others. I participated in NaHaiWriMo the following year and also went on to get published in myriad haiku, haiga, and haibun journals. I was beginning to carve a niche for myself and started my own literary & arts journal, *Sonic Boom*, in December 2014, which contains a section devoted to Japanese short-forms of poetry. I also co-edited *naad anunaad: an anthology of contemporary world haiku* (Vishwakarma Publications, 2016) along with Kala Ramesh and Sanjuktaa Asopa, for which I was awarded "Promising Haijin and Editor" by the *IN Haiku* community at the Triveni World Haiku Utsav in 2016. Apart from writing haiku, I also enjoy creating erasures and found poems, singing, and creating minimalist/abstract art in my free time. My poems and artworks have been published in over 200 print and online venues of repute, and one of my remixed poems was nominated for the *Best of the Net* anthology in 2015.

rea
ding
again
st th
e gra
in a cr
ow's win
gbe
at

bones 14

rain check   the shelf life of opportunities

Frameless Sky 7

in teentaal the remainder of my dream sequence

Under the Basho 2017

the mutation of ideas in sweater weather

failed haiku 18

either/or
i relapse into
a coda

bones 14

self-validation
raindrops on a telephone wire

failed haiku 23

Name **Adelaide B. Shaw**
Volume *A New Resonance* 3
Residence **Millbrook NY**
Occupation **Retired Legal Assistant**
Collection *An Unknown Road*

Since appearing in *A New Resonance* 3 I have published one collection of haiku, *An Unknown Road* (Modern English Tanka Press, 2009) which came in third in the Mildred Kanterman Merit Book Awards. I have been a judge for the Merit Awards (2014) and for other contests, including tanka and haibun. In 2015 I won first place in the Peggy Willis Lyles *Heron's Nest* contest, have placed well in other contests and have often been a featured artist for my haiga on *Haigaonline*. Other published writing includes book reviews and articles. In 2008 I began a blog of my published work. Haiku has always been a way for me to record experiences in such a way that the moment immediately comes back. Being clear and concise without being subjective is the challenge of the form. With the difficulties that come with aging and other life changes haiku continues to provide an outlet in writing and an inspiration and pleasure in reading. Although my creative endeavors include tanka, tanka prose, haibun, and haiga, I always come back to haiku for the discipline, the control, the need to be observant, the exactness and the intensity of the moment.

spring equinox
a change in the melody
of melting ice
Peggy Willis Lyles Contest 2015
1st Place

coffee in a mug
warming my hands
yours over mine
The Heron's Nest XIX:1

the day's heat
flowing up to the stars
"Rhapsody in Blue"
Acorn 39

moonless sky
the deep night speaks
with many voices
Presence 55

stone chapel
the echo of a heavy door
thudding to a close
Modern Haiku 45.3

autumn garden
gathering this and that
for a last display
Frogpond 34.2

Name	Sandra Simpson
Volume	*A New Resonance* 5
Residence	Tauranga New Zealand
Occupation	Publicist/Programmer
Collection	*breath*

breath, my first (and so far only) collection, was published in 2012. Recent major awards include: First and Third, 2017 Martin Lucas Haiku Award (UK); Second, 2016 Martin Lucas Haiku Award; First, 2015 *Free XpresSion* Haiku Contest (Australia); Second, 2013 *Haiku Presence* Award (UK); First, 2013 Royal Canal Haiku Contest (Ireland); Second, 2013 NZ Poetry Society International Haiku Contest; Second, 2013 *Haiku Magazine* Contest (Romania); Favourite Haiku in 2013 *The Heron's Nest* Readers' Choice Awards; Second, 2012 Janice Bostok Haiku Award (Australia); First, 2012 *Free XpresSion* Haiku Contest. I am secretary of the Katikati Haiku Pathway committee and editor of the online *Haiku NewZ*. In 2012 Margaret Beverland and I organised a Haiku Festival Aotearoa in Tauranga and in 2018 I will co-edit, with Margaret, a Fourth *NZ Haiku Anthology*. I am a wife, and mother to two adult children. For fun I grow orchids and play badminton, read, go for walks, garden and photograph plants. I have visited Japan twice and would very much like to return.

    wet spring —
    in a box by the fire
    a small bleat
        Presence 59

    only my face
    above water
    moonrise
        building a time machine

undulating through elephant grass the day's first water jars
    The Mamba 2

    in a cabinet marked Mesopotamia a broken face
        HaikuNow! Haiku Contest 2011
        Runner-Up

    Christmas eve —
    the pop-up book's manger
    missing its baby
        Martin Lucas Haiku Award 2016
        2nd Place

    summer solstice —
    pulling the earth
    back round a zinnia
        Robert Spiess Memorial Haiku Contest 2017
        2nd Place

Name **Brendan Slater**
Volume ***A New Resonance* 9**
Residence **Stoke-on-Trent England**
Occupation **Unemployed Rat Catcher**

Ku and all the new forms derived by the imagists from the Japanese originals starting at the beginning of the 20th century and continuing to this day, and the English language versions of the Japanese short forms such as tanka and haibun, etc, are so misunderstood they have, in some circles, become a cheap joke, with haiku being regularly compared to limericks. These tiny poetic expressions are packed like the universe before the big bang: unimaginably dense yet infinitesimally small, containing all the mass of the universe yet weightless. They should be handled with care, and it is our job, all of us who write these forms, to write and publish as much as possible. So magazines, e-zines, journals, self-published books, whatever you need to do to get your work published, do it. However, the need for an editorial process is vital and should never be skipped. Even the best poets have off days. I am not sure I can add anything about my personal life because most of my poems are written about it.

night rain fills the
skip i hide
in shallow
thoughts
Hedgerow 74

city night
the gangster
tightens his hood
Pirene's Fountain 4.9

Betamax clouds of cellophane unwrap
otoliths 38

through mathematical mist a father
otoliths 43

the sound
of my own voice
wild honey
Notes from the Gean 2.4

before dawn
the ancient language
of a cat's tail
Notes from the Gean 1.4

Name **William Sorlien**
Volume ***A New Resonance* 9**
Residence **woods & river MN**
Occupation **Pamphleteer**

The question often arises, "do any of our efforts make a difference?" To do so would be to imply a single-mindedness, something of universal appeal and with a solidarity of purpose. Yet haiku has a solitary nature, at least in the composition. They are singularly our own, ego and emotion conveyed in the briefest manner; the time it takes to expel a breath. Yet succinct as they are, our words derive from a multitude of views and environments. How then do we relate to one another? A certain Ms Warther of the winsome smile might relate it best; "Far-flung indeed! My goal is to continue flinging, if you will, in all directions, allowing it to stick where it will. One never knows. Yet, of the power of short verse, I have no doubt." Most of my poems are real time accounts of experiences I enjoy (or suffer). Often alluding to some social commentary. If they should ever sound or lean to the surreal, well, that's because it is, though I prefer to call life simply Absurd. A daunting endeavor, you might ask? I revel in the irony and humor, especially when I can laugh at myself. Obviously, we don't prosper alone, either. I owe a great debt to two outstanding mentors, Lorin Ford and John Carley. It would be a disservice not to at least mention their names, for their work and for their contributions to the way.

the tall corn's shadow
falls across the grave yard —
Autumn is coming
unpublished

tall grass, dry and amber —
I release the cicada
I kept in a jar
unpublished

reading Fujitsu
to Chet Baker tunes —
light snow in April
unpublished

today's moon —
these gewgaws in my pockets
find a semiotic niche
unpublished

winter is near —
I call my jacket
by its name
unpublished

moon flies and chigger bugs
circle 'round the porch light —
Dad calls us all in
unpublished

Name **Melissa Spurr**
Volume *A New Resonance* 7
Residence **Joshua Tree CA**
Occupation **Marketing Specialist**

No update.

> taking and giving
> the morning light
> cherry blossoms
>> Cherry Blossom Contest 2009

what we don't speak of —
the rain-soaked gate
swollen shut
> *The Heron's Nest* XII:3

> motel room
> passing headlights change
> the shape of darkness
>> HaikuNow! Contest 2010

autumn love
letting him feel
my scar
> Shiki Kukai 2010

> the way
> he still looks at me
> purple sage
>> *Frogpond* 33.3

shortest day
snow drifting higher
on the sundial
> *Notes from the Gean* 1.2

Name **R. A. Stefanac**
Volume *A New Resonance* 1
Residence **Pittsburgh PA**
Occupation **Gallery Manager**

No update.

                hunter's moon
                the overflow crowd
                at the singles bar
                    RAW NerVZ V:3

Christmas past
the pine needles
under the rug
    Woodnotes 27

                adding weight
                to the bending peony —
                black ants
                    Modern Haiku 33.2

steady rain
a crossing guard
hunches her shoulders
    black bough 11

                dad's wake
                  the weight
                of my new shoes
                    Mayfly 22

alone . . .
a downdraft
stirs the ashes
    Sooouth by Southeast 4.1

Name **Gary Steinberg**
Volume ***A New Resonance* 3**
Residence **Mahwah NJ**
Occupation **Soccer Mom**

No update.

>> november rain
>> the suicide bridge
>> sheeted in ice
>>> *RAW NeerVZ* VIII:3

cemetery wind the cellophane of fresh flowers crinkles
> *Frogpond* 24.2

>> winter rain I finger each seam on the baseball
>>> *Frogpond* 24.2

winter night perfection before my first syllable
> *RAW NeerVZ* VIII:4

>> the sound of sleet when there's nothing left to say
>>> *Frogpond* 23.2

> shooting star
> all my wishes
> she makes for me
>> *RAW NeerVZ* VIII:4

Name **Lucas Stensland**
Volume *A New Resonance* 8
Residence **Tampa FL**
Occupation **Senior Manager Corporate Law Firm**
Collections *my favorite thing*
fun again

My collections *my favorite thing* (co-written with Bob Lucky and Michael Ketchek) and *Fun Again* have both been on the shortlist for the Touchstone Book Award.

how long
she holds the umbrella
after the rain
Frogpond 35.3

domestic dispute
the cat interrupts us
to ask for a treat
Haibun Today 10

mix tape
how I said
good bye
Shamrock 17

winter rain
a child finds
his lost toy
Haibun Today 10

a bartender
I don't recognize
knows my drink
Prune Juice 6

Name **Carmen Sterba**
Volume *A New Resonance* 4
Residence **University Place WA**
Occupation **College Instructor**
Collections *sunlit jar*
An Amazement of Deer

In 2011, Judt Shrode, Jim Westenhaver, and I founded the Commencement Bay Haiku group in Tacoma. Besides meeting monthly, we were invited by a library to inspire homeschooled children to write haiku in our area. In 2015, I gave a power point presentation on "Keeping Touch with International Poets" at Haiku Northwest's Seabeck Getaway. At Haiku North America at Santa Fe in 2017, I gave a reading of my new chapbook, *An Amazement of Deer: In Haiku, Photos, Narratives, and Solo Rengay*. I retired one year ago from a career of teaching ESL in Japanese and American colleges. I continue to help immigrants or international students with English by volunteering at my local library. Now I look forward to more time to keep composing better haiku.

seaside town
I long to walk
on clouds again
on down the road

4th of July
nostalgia for fireflies
on the opposite coast
Acorn 39

day moon
knowing I overstayed
my welcome
The Heron's Nest XIX:2

that long-ago child . . .
pounding nasturtium petals
with a rock
Seabeck Anthology 2016

sherwood forest
under the flicker's wings
a flash of gold
A Hundred Gourds 5.3

Name Jeff Stillman
Volume *A New Resonance* 6
Residence FL / NY
Occupation Retired Elem Teacher
Collections *Past Due*
small blessings
autumn deepening

My first haiku collection *Past Due* was published by Red Moon Press in 2015. I work on haiku almost daily, spend a lot of time at the gym and on my rowing machine — and as much time as I can with my two young grandsons. I enjoy surf casting in south Florida.

spindly branches' last leaves clinging to each other
    Modern Haiku 47.3

raging blizzard
the gritted teeth
of jumper cables
    The Heron's Nest XIV:1

Father's Day fishing . . .
his lure
still dances
    Acorn 38

first warm day
kettle bells prop open
the gym doors
    Modern Haiku 48.3

rippling cloud shadow   what passes for a back story
    Frogpond 40.1

Name: Richard S. Straw
Volume: *A New Resonance* 6
Residence: Cary NC
Occupation: Technical Copyeditor

In the late 1980s, I edited *Pine Needles*, a quarterly newsletter for the North Carolina Haiku Society. In 1988, I compiled *late afternoon bum*, a trifold Haiku Canada Sheet. I self-published in 2001 *A Hiker Sees His Shadow*, an eight-page haiku sequence dedicated to the memory of my dad, then in 2005 put together another haiku trifold, *Opening a Window*. In the spring of 2009, I printed *The Longest Time*, a collection of 35 of my haibun that had been published in haiku and haibun journals between 2006 and 2009. Since then, I've been working on an expanded edition of that collection, excerpts of which appear in *Journeys 2017: An Anthology of International Haibun*, edited by Angelee Deodhar. Writing haibun (and haiku) is like sharing memories with an old friend over a coffee or tea or sometimes like talking (or wishing I could talk) on the phone with someone in my family who's moved far away. Each describes or tries to explain a living and (it is hoped) truthful feeling. Rather than puzzle anyone, I've tried to share only what I've experienced, which was simple enough, as it must be for most.

late for church
from an open barn door
the lowing of cows

The Heron's Nest XI:2

drenched by a shower
drying out
in a basement barroom

Frogpond 40.2

sunlit lectern
the family Bible open
to *Ecclesiastes*

Haibun Today 11.2

still pitch black
a mockingbird's rehearsal
of a new song

Bolin Brook Farm Anthology 2012

emptying trees
against a harvest moon
vacancy

Frogpond 40.2

end of a year
my dead father's watch
keeping time still

Contemporary Haibun Online 13.1

Name **André Surridge**
Volume ***A New Resonance* 7**
Residence **Hamilton New Zealand**
Occupation **Retired**

I remain indebted to the late Cyril Childs for showing me the haiku way at a workshop in Petone in 2002. Over one thousand of my haiku and senryu have been published since that time and I am still learning. I have won several international awards including the *paper wasp* Jack Stamm Haiku Award, 2006; Jane Reichhold International Prize 2010 & 2011; Janice Bostok International Haiku Award, 2012. I was diagnosed with AML (Acute Myeloid Leukemia) in February 2017. Thankfully I'm currently in remission. Married to my lovely wife, Timmy for 34 years. We live at the Summerset Retirement Village in Hamilton, New Zealand.

      the softness
      of lamb's ears
      garden for the blind
         The Heron's Nest XIV:1

years later
still catching in her throat
the taste of ash
   paper wasp 19.1

reminding me I am dust this shaft of sunlight
  Valley Micropress 16.1

      steepled fingers she talks about the broken cathedral
        Kokako 21

    when it seems
    winter will never end
    plum blossom
      Presence 57

end of chemo
in a soft brush the last
of his hair
  Pulse May 2017

Name **Hilary Tann**
Volume *A New Resonance* 8
Residence Schuylerville NY
Occupation Composer/Music Professor

Since 2013, my poems have appeared in The *Heron's Nest* (Editor's Choice, December 2017), *Modern Haiku*, and Mann Library's *Daily Haiku*. I was delighted to be included in the anthology *Another Country: Haiku Poetry from Wales* (Gomer Press, ed. Nigel Jenkins, Ken Jones, Lynne Rees). In Fall 2015, together with Co-Director John Stevenson, we hosted HNA2015 at Union College where I chair the Department of Music. My 17-year association with the Biannual Anthology of Haiku and Senryu, *Upstate Dim Sum*, continues to be a source of joy and companionship (John Stevenson, Yu Chang, Tom Clausen, and haiga artist Ion Codrescu). My personal life is primarily that of a composer. I write orchestral, chamber, and choral music. I look forward to devoting my time to nature, music, and haiku when I retire from college teaching in June 2019.

silence
for some
includes birdsong
The Heron's Nest XIX:4

late fall
a skeleton cradles
a pumpkin
Modern Haiku 49.1

evening walk spirits of former dogs
The Heron's Nest XVIII:1

spring flowers each leaf a blade
Modern Haiku 47.3

my own tides —
tug of the
near moon
The Heron's Nest XIX:1

old hymns —
posts and beams
intertwined
The Heron's Nest XVII:4

Name **Dietmar Tauchner**
Volume *A New Resonance* 5
Residence Puchberg Austria
Occupation Author/Social Worker
Collections *as far as i can*
noise of our origin
invisible tracks

Some of my awards include Taisho (Grand Prize) at the International Kusamakura Haiku Competition in Kumamoto, Japan, 2013; 1st Prize at the Haiku International Association (HIA) Award in Tokyo, Japan 2008, 2011 and 2014; 2nd Place for *noise of our origin* from the Mildred Kanterman Merit Book Awards (Haiku Society of America, 2014). I am the founder of the Haiku Journal *Chrysanthemum* and a member of the *Red Moon Anthology* Editorial Staff since 2013. My books (in English) include *as far as i can* (Red Moon Press, 2010); *noise of our origin* (Red Moon Press, 2013); *invisible tracks* (Red Moon Press, 2015); and I am included in *Haiku in English: The First 100 Years* (W.W. Norton, 2013). As to my personal life — well, I try to express my experiences & awareness in my poems . . .

new radio
noise
of our origin
noise of our origin

spring night
i offer my genes
to a stranger
dust devils

southbound birds the loop of identity
invisible tracks

snow in the creator's synapses
NOON 10

a molecule
of the milky way
. . . home moon
Modern Haiku 47.3

starry night
i become an icon
of windsong
Blithe Spirit 27.3

Name	Petar Tchouhov
Volume	*A New Resonance* 5
Residence	Sofia Bulgaria
Occupation	Librarian
Collection	*Safety Pins*

I started writing haiku about 20 years ago. Over all these years I have published my poems in many Bulgarian and international anthologies and magazines online and in print such as *The Red Moon Anthology of English-Language Haiku* (2006, 2007, 2008, 2009), *Simply Haiku, The Heron's Nest, Full Moon, Roadrunner, tinywords, Frogpond, Modern Haiku, bottle rockets, Contemporary Haibun, Haiku Presence, Magnapoets, Ginyu, World Haiku, Mainichi Daily News*, and others. My first book of haiku *Safety Pins* was published in 2010 in Bulgarian and English and was translated into Gaelic and published in Ireland in 2012 (*Bioráin Dhúnta*, Original Writing, Dublin). I have participated in many haiku festivals and conferences in Bulgaria and abroad. For my haiku I received the top prize at the 61st Basho Festival in Japan (2007), the second prize at the 1st International Facebook Haiku Contest (2010), and several awards at the 5th International Haiku Contest, Moscow, Russia (2012) among others. Other than haiku I write poetry, prose and drama and have published 10 poetry books, a novel, a collection of short stories and a play. I also write music and lyrics and have played the guitar in different rock bands. I am a great beer lover, so   cheers!

falling leaf
I'm drawing
my family trees
Safety Pins

winter night
a sudden rhyme
in the blank verse
World Haiku 2018

new moon
someone else will hear
my words for you
Modern Haiku 43.3

torrential rain —
for all who are
ashamed to cry
World Haiku 2016

Christmas Eve
I change Santa Claus'
old battery
Catalyst 13

so far away
from Mount Fuji —
a dead snail
The Haiku of Kobayashi Issa
May 2010

Name **Michelle Tennison**
Volume *A New Resonance* 9
Residence **Blackwood NJ**
Occupation **Writer / Teacher**
Collection *murmuration*

Author of *murmuration* with Red Moon Press, 2016, and *A Lit Jellyfish*, a collaborative blog based on a surrealist literary game. Currently teaching haiku online. Throughout my life I have sought ways to apply my sensitivity as a gift, and I have found that haiku as a poetry of insight offers a wonderful path and opportunity in that regard. About a decade ago I experienced a sudden intuitive awakening that continues to inform my life and work.

whale song
I become
an empty boat
Acorn 32

nectar
&
eyes
on
wings
to
pass
through
death
Frogpond 38.2

fireflies
& soul
fragments
is/let 29 January 2015

her breath where a sea begins
Modern Haiku 47.1

mother the slow rhythmic pulse of swan wings
Roadrunner 12.3

raven shadow clinging tightly to my victim story
Modern Haiku 43.2

Name	Scott Terrill
Volume	*A New Resonance* 9
Residence	Melbourne Australia
Occupation	Yoga Teacher
Collection	*Southern Humpback*

My ku have been described as similar to direct English language translations of Japanese haiku along with all the strange grammatical anomalies one might expect. I like that. I also like to play around with tense, it feels joyous somehow. I have a couple of books published through Yet To Be Named Free Press as well as appearing in a number of anthologies, notably *A New Resonance* 9. I am currently teaching yoga through my business *the yogi practice*.

surrounded
by the smell of asparagus
a house in mourning
NOON 10

down to the sea breeze
earthworms and the childless
are identical
bones 8

A-bomb manga
falling through
the dead pixel
bones 8

for a fleeting moment
a crab becomes a god
hunting sideways
Frogpond 37.3

humpback moon
in a half-built scraper
a light flickers on and on
Per Diem 2014

passing through
the amber of pregnant horses
a winter galaxy
Frogpond 37.3

Name **Tony A. Thompson**
Volume ***A New Resonance* 6**
Residence **Lufkin TX**
Occupation **Law Enforcement**

No update.

                        first in the cemetery winter violets
                                 White Lotus 7

sharpening the blade heat shimmer
   A New Resonance 6

                        wind shift
                        she casts
                        where he did
                              Acorn 21

      the long day
      rain water seeps over
      the top of the barrel
          Riverbed 1

                        family reunion
                        a table cloth pops
                        in the wind
                              The Heron's Nest 7.3

      alone at dusk
      the old woman still
      pulling weeds
            bottle rockets 18

Name Jennie Townsend
Volume *A New Resonance* 4
Residence O'Fallon MO
Occupation Oncology Nurse

No update.

        strawberry moon
        another storm stalls
        at the river
           A New Resonance 4

july heat —
scrubbing just smears
the crayon
   A New Resonance 4

        the wind picks up —
        I finger the creases
        of a letter in my pocket
           A New Resonance 4

summer afternoon
the boys tell stories
about someday
   The Heron's Nest V:11

        she tucks his letter
        into the folded flag
        on Independence Day
           A New Resonance 4

autumn blue —
he reaches the mailbox
on tiptoes
   A New Resonance 4

Name **Els van Leeuwen**
Volume ***A New Resonance* 10**
Residence **Sydney Australia**
Occupation **Early Childhood Educator**

I always longed to write poetry, but usually found I could only write quite short succinct pieces that didn't develop beyond a few lines in the way I believed a poem was supposed to. Then, ten years ago, I discovered haiku, and have been indulging a quiet passion for reading and writing it ever since. Surprisingly, I seem to get my little poems published reasonably regularly in quite respectful journals, for which I am grateful. I rarely enter competitions or aim for much more. It is enough for me to share my work with other enthusiasts in the good company I find in these journals. I am in a busy and demanding season of my life, raising a family and working full time. My love for haiku reminds me to look around, take a breath and soak up the beauty and depth in the world around me. I am blessed to be married to another writer of haiku, who encourages and supports me to make time to nourish my poetic sensibility and keep writing, no matter how much we have going on in our lives.

summer's end
the quality
of moonlight on film
HaikuOz Website July 2017

the tired face
on a doll house figure
yet another heatwave
Modern Haiku 48.3

evening glow
the security door
propped open
Modern Haiku 48.2

ripe persimmons
the ladder left standing
in the tree
Contemporary Haibun Online 13.2

a child's grave
without a name
my face in the river
Modern Haiku 48.1

lit ship
on the night horizon
no reply
Frogpond 40.1

Name **Julie Warther**
Volume ***A New Resonance*** 9
Residence **Dover OH**
Occupation **Writer**
Collection ***What Was Here***

Since appearing in *A New Resonance* 9, I have enjoyed volunteering in the haiku community. As Midwest Regional Coordinator for the Haiku Society of America, I have promoted haiku in the region by presenting at regional and national poetry meetings, installing a Forest Haiku Path which features 26 Midwest poets, and facilitating the Ohaio-Ku Study Group. In addition, I serve on the editorial boards for *Red Moon Anthology*, Touchstone Book Awards, and *Living Senryu Anthology*. My first chapbook, *What Was Here*, was published in 2015 by Folded Word Press. While I continue to write and submit haiku, I particularly enjoy collaborating with haiku friends on rengay and tan renga. My goal is to continue to share the beauty of haiku and encourage new writers of the form.

moonbeam . . .
holding a picture
that can't hold back
Modern Haiku 48.1

loaves and fishes
this thin slice
of moon
Wild Plum Spring/Summer 2017

just before dawn the barn swallows the bats
Kaji Aso Contest 2017
Honorable Mention

after the last cherry blossom leaves
Wild Plum 3.2

support group . . .
the comfort of the chair
between us
Mariposa 37

wildflowers . . .
great are the affairs
of bees
Tinywords 16.1

Name **Paul Watsky**
Volume *A New Resonance* 1
Residence **SF Bay Area CA**
Occupation **Jungian Analyst**
Collections *Telling the Difference*
Walk-Up Music

My career as a haiku poet lasted about seven years, and aside from translating ended about twenty years ago, when I returned to writing longer, occidental forms of poetry. During that earlier period I appeared in several *Red Moon Anthologies*, a Two Autumns chapbook, and was awarded second place two successive years in the Brady competition. More recently I have partnered with Emiko Miyashita in a book-length translation of Santoka (PIE Books, 2006), and again in 2016 when we collaborated in translating 10 haiku each from four contemporary Japanese haijin, published in a collection of current Japanese verse: haiku, tanka, and long poems, which appeared in *Jung Journal: Culture and Psyche* (Winter, 2016), for which Emiko served as one of two guest poetry editors. Over the past ten years two collections of my more recent poems have been published: *Telling The Difference* (2010) and *Walk-Up Music* (2015), the latter receiving a recommended review from Kirkus. I also have spent the past five years serving as poetry editor of *Jung Journal*, a quarterly published by Taylor and Francis. My twin sons, whose childhood energy made it impossible for me to concentrate on longer verse forms, are now in their thirties, Simon a pilot who flies an air ambulance, and George a rapper and poet. I remain busy with my psychotherapy practice, and am currently vice president of the San Francisco Jung Institute.

from the mirage
a hand comes out and grabs
the rice ball
    Takano Mutsuo
    Jung Journal: Culture and Psyche, Winter 2016

snow falling
on the mud's so beautiful —
turns into mud
    Ogawa Keishu
    Jung Journal: Culture and Psyche, Winter 2016

no one picks up
no one steps on
the black leather glove
    Tsugawa Eriko
    Jung Journal: Culture and Psyche, Winter 2016

wheat's autumn —
every last grain
rotting in the sea
    Terui Midori
    Jung Journal: Culture and Psyche, Winter 2016

Name: Harriot West
Volume: *A New Resonance* 5
Residence: Eugene OR
Occupation: Writer / Editor
Collection: *Into the Light*

Highlights include the publication of my first book, *Into the Light*, which was a co-first place winner of the 2015 HSA Merit Book Award; the Museum of Haiku Literature Award; being featured in the Spotlight in *Modern Haiku*; and three *Modern Haiku* awards for best haibun. My work appears in journals including *Frogpond, Haibun Today, KYSO Flash, Contemporary Haibun Online*, and various anthologies including *Haiku in English: The First Hundred Years, Contemporary Haibun, Red Moon Anthology* and *Best Small Fictions 2017*. I am a founding member of the Eugene Haiku group and am currently at work on two new collections of haibun and tanka prose. When I first began studying/writing haiku I ordered volumes 1-4 of *A New Resonance* — never imaging I would one day be invited to join the ranks. Being dubbed 'emerging' at the age of 60 remains one of my favorite haiku moments. My new collection of haibun and tanka prose, *Shades of Absence*, will be published in 2018.

day moon
one of us has
nothing to do
Modern Haiku 46.2

Auld Lang Syne
a desire to straighten
the stranger's tie
Modern Haiku 43.1

casual embrace —
suddenly conscious
of my breasts
Modern Haiku 43.1

blue sky
maybe I don't need
to be right
Acorn 23

dusk
the girl we didn't like
with fireflies in her hair
Presence 36

releasing him . . .
the bull trout's back
scarred by talons
The Heron's Nest XII:3

Name	Dick Whyte
Volume	*A New Resonance* 10
Residence	Te Whanganui-a-Tara, Aotearoa
Occupation	Lecturer
Collections	*A Book of Sparrows*
	A Book of Seasons

I have been writing haiku for around 10 years. I worked as an editor for *Haiku News* with Laurence Stacey, and we released an anthology of work published through the journal. Since then I have published two books of my work (*A Book of Sparrows*, 2016; *A Book of Seasons*, 2017), and a small book of translations of 1600s Japanese haiku, in collaboration with Emiko Sheehan, who illustrated and selected the poems (*Sitting Nose To Nose*, 2017). I am currently working on cataloguing English translations of *haikai* from 1700 – 1850, for a series of upcoming projects.

sunrise,
the sparrows sing
for no-one
A Book of Seasons

seagulls
making a racket . . .
hazy moon
A Book of Seasons

dead sparrow
ruffling its feathers . . .
summer wind
A Book of Seasons

last light
brushing your cheek . . .
against mine
A Book of Seasons

the birds
never seem lost . . .
autumn sky
A Book of Seasons

from me
to the mountain—
first frost
A Book of Seasons

Name Billie Wilson
Volume *A New Resonance* 3
Residence Juneau AK
Occupation Retired Paralegal

I am an associate editor for *The Heron's Nest*, coordinate the annual haiku competition honoring Robert Spiess, and manage the Haiku Registry for The Haiku Foundation. Some of my haiku have been recognized with awards from the Haiku Society of America, the Snapshot Press *Haiku Calendar* Competition, *The Heron's Nest* Readers' Choice Poem of the Year, and others. My work is included in *Haiku in English: The First Hundred Years*, *Where the River Goes*, several *Red Moon Anthologies*, and others. I was a guest reader at the Haiku Poets of Northern California's annual Two Autumns Reading and a Guest Poet for the *Upstate Dim Sum* haiku journal. I am one of 45 poets whose work was selected for the video/computer game *Haiku Journey*. For many years, I served as the Haiku Society of America's Regional Coordinator for Alaska. My first haiku collection is forthcoming from Snapshot Press. I spent my childhood in rural Indiana, moving in 1962 to Alaska when my first attempts at writing haiku began. I have two sons; my husband Gary has a son and a daughter; and we share 11 grandchildren and three great-grandchildren.

that whale I could have touched
surfaces again
in my mind
Mariposa 15

rattlesnake country
shadows of storm clouds
darken the foothills
Mariposa 19

campfire sparks —
someone outside the circle
starts another song
The Heron's Nest XII:2

Bohemian waxwings —
and I didn't even have
a bucket list
Close to the Wind

truck stop
we try to imagine
what Lewis and Clark saw
Muttering Thunder 2

the eons I was not here
the eons I won't be
winter stars
Acorn 37

Name **Jeffrey Winke**
Volume *A New Resonance 2*
Residence **Milwaukee WI**
Occupation **Writer**
Collections *What's Not There*
Against Natural Impulse
Vexing Laughter
That Smirking Face

No update.

> waking to
> the daily sameness —
> shoes neatly paired
> _{*What's Not There*}

airport runway grass —
watching it blow
in all directions
_{*What's Not There*}

> gray day
> the air thick
> with lilacs
> _{*What's Not There*}

chalk outline
where the body was
last warm night
_{*What's Not There*}

> peak autumn color —
> appreciating those few
> green leaves
> _{*What's Not There*}

cold snap
steam slowly rises
from the sewage pond
_{*What's Not There*}

Name **Laura Young**
Volume *A New Resonance* 1
Residence Monticello FL
Occupation Materials Creator

No update.

        with each crash
        the sound of the chain saw
        clearer
            A New Resonance 1

the answering machine
playing mother's voice too slowly —
    winter light
        A New Resonance 1

        month of night —
        a neighbor reading mail
        by carlight
            A New Resonance 1

the short day —
a woodpile grows
on the porch
    A New Resonance 1

        firelight —
        thawing out the top layer
        of their wedding cake
            A New Resonance 1

time to dig
the sweet potatoes
still no news from you
    A New Resonance 1

Name   **Quendryth Young**
Volume   *A New Resonance* 7
Residence **Alstonville Australia**
Occupation **Retired Cytologist**
Collection *The Whole Body Singing*

Haiku became my passion when I was sixty nine, and since then over 1000 of my haiku have been published in twelve countries and six languages, earning twenty major international awards. My ongoing role as coordinator of Cloudcatchers, a group of haiku poets on the Far North Coast of NSW, began in 2005, conducting seasonal ginko and email round-robins (forty-nine so far). I was associated with the fostering of Australian haiku on-line in Wollumbin Haiku Workshop (2006 – 2009), and edited the inaugural haiku section of *FreeXpresSion* (2007 – 2009). *The Whole Body Singing* was placed second in the Mildred Kanterman Memorial Book Awards (HSA, 2008), and I received a Touchstone Award (THF) in 2010. Highlights have been the presentation of a paper at The Fourth Pacific Rim Haiku Conference in 2009, and then an inspirational In the Footsteps of Basho tour of Japan in 2010. Scott Mason, in *The Wonder Code* (2017) promotes my on-line Haiku Workshop as 'incisive yet friendly'. I cherish my husband of fifty-seven years, two children and five grandchildren. My career of over forty years as a cytologist (studying Pap smears, body fluids and fine needle aspirations), involved research and the publication of three scientific papers relating to 'The Detection of Adenocarcinoma of the Cervix Uteri'. In 1973 I placed first when the International Academy of Cytology conducted its inaugural examinations in Australia, and the following year was invited to become a member of the Academy. Another on-going passion since 1980 has been playing Bridge (National Master **), with additional enthusiasm for choral singing, ikebana, family history and bird watching.

her body
laid to rest . . .
indigo violet
Presence 59

headstone
my face reflected
in the plaque
The Heron's Nest XVIII:2

all eyes
wide open
aquarium
Kusamakura Haiku Contest 2016

a peg
in the dryer . . .
this foetus
Modern Haiku 45.1

a wake of dust
follows the reaper
autumn twilight
Frogpond 36.3

burning cane
a pathway of smoke
to the moon
Muttering Thunder 1

Name **J. Zimmerman**
Volume ***A New Resonance* 8**
Residence **Santa Cruz CA**
Occupation **Archaeometrist**

I was the first poet-in-residence for the Cabrillo Festival of Contemporary Music (2014). I give haiku, tanka, and haibun workshops on a volunteer basis for Yuki Teikei Haiku Society. Occasionally review books and write essays for *Modern Haiku*. Book reviewer for *Ribbons* (Tanka Society of America). Best-of-issue haibun award for "Credo" (*Modern Haiku* 48:1). Second prize for "Ah Morelia" in the Tanka Society of America first tanka prose contest in 2015. A *Daily Haiku* poet 2015 – 2016. I saw totality of the 2017 Total Solar Eclipse. Started attending a kick-bottom lunch-time cross-training gym class. Complete 17-mile day hikes now and then, sometimes on the same day as I began. Completely flummoxed in attempting to learn Japanese (loss rate exceeds acquisition rate). Still cannot sing.

finding my place
in the asperger's spectrum
winter rainbow
Frogpond

probing
the wound
winter light
Modern Haiku

shadow bands
the soft conversation
of owls
Acorn

slinging her school scarf
over her shoulder the rush
into winter
GEPPO

sitting zazen
in the firewatcher's seat
smoke-colored robes
Presence 47

mirage
we walk all day
into the future
tinywords

The Editors

Name **Jim Kacian**
Residence **Winchester VA**
Occupation **Poet / Publisher**
Collections *Presents of Mind*
Six Directions
long after
after image

A New Resonance has been one of the most pleasurable and rewarding things with which I have been involved in my nearly four decades in haiku. This is due not only to my close work with so many wonderful poets, but also for the two decades of discovery and companionship with my fellow editor Dee Evetts.

> late summer
> after the **scab**
> the
>
> *Modern Haiku* 45.1

Name **Dee Evetts**
Residence **Winchester VA**
Occupation **Bookbinder**
Collection *endgrain*

It is my privilege to have been closely involved with this unique project, that has now spanned two decades, and to have spent innumerable Saturday afternoons debating with my co-editor Jim Kacian the merits of this poem or that — at times beside the fire in winter and other times out of doors in spring — and thereby have become acquainted with a remarkable range of personalities and talents.

> morning sneeze
> the guitar in the corner
> resonates
>
> Harold E. Henderson Haiku Contest 1990